ONCE UPON A TIME IN THE DUST:

Burning Man Around the World

by Roxane Jessi

Once Upon a Time in the Dust
Burning Man Around the World

First paperback edition March 2023
Published by Burning Man Project, San Francisco USA

Cover design by Dominic "DA" Tinio
Cover photo by Roxane Jessi
Cover Artwork: *San Clan* (AfrikaBurn)

ISBN 978-1-7349659-4-0 (paperback)
ISBN 978-1-7349659-5-7 (eBook)

www.roxanejessi.com
www.burningman.org

To all those who dream of better worlds

and take part in their creation.

And those who live life as a story to be told.

Contents

Introduction

My first Burn was a whirlwind. I had arrived shattered and skeptical, and spent the first day disoriented, wondering what the fuss was about. Had this just been an expensive trip to a dustbowl of hippies in the middle of nowhere? 48 hours later my mind had been blown to pieces by the humanity and playfulness I found in every interaction, and I was tearing up with joy watching people dancing freely in the sunrise, lost in the moment. I had never experienced anything like this before. It was 2015, and one of the dustiest, coldest Burns in recent years, with never-ending whiteouts during the day and temperatures below freezing every night, but somehow through those epic dust storms I emerged a different person.

It shook up all my beliefs, tore apart my 15-year relationship and set me on a journey wherein I left the big city, quit my office job, started working remotely, and tried to unplug from the grid. It was like pressing the reset button on life, but I couldn't quite put my finger on exactly why.

When I first set about writing this book I was stuck in a rut, living in one of the most fast-paced and disconnected cities in the world. Sitting in a packed tube to go to work every morning I noticed how tired and unhappy people looked—gray versions of themselves in gray suits, flipping through their phones mindlessly in the rush hour without exchanging a word. I thought about how our modern cities are stunting us as social and expressive beings.

The Burning Man phenomenon turns this world on its head. It is a hub of effervescent creativity, of connection, of community, where no currency exchanges hands for a week, but we feel so much richer coming out of it. I didn't know how this fit into the life I had constructed.

I just knew I wanted to narrow the time between Burns.

Three Burns later I decided to do just that. I would immerse myself in this world, traveling to one Burn per continent over the course of a year, to try to understand what made people around the world connect with the Burner values across widely different cultures. What did creating a pop-up community mean in these varied contexts, and how was it channeled through art, self-expression, ritual, and the interactions of participants?

I was excited to research a movement that brings people together and speaks of communal effort and civic responsibility at a time when the world is increasingly disconnected. For over a decade I have been working in the international aid sector, based on replicating capitalist models of society in contexts that are not set up for it. The year after my first Burn, 2016, was a year where politics and people polarized; the world seemed to be turning bleaker, and the media stories more depressing. But in the midst of this chaos, undercurrents like the Burn helped to shine a light on a system that seems archaic, consumerist, pits us against each other, and silences creativity. These undercurrents show us another way.

Today the Burn movement is emerging from the shadows of counterculture into the mainstream. But the growth hasn't all been smooth, and in the throes of the Instagram generation, the principles that defined it are now in question. The increasing commodification of a community which champions decommodification has given rise to community dialogues about Burning Man's identity. These have grown more urgent since the founder and mastermind of Burning Man, Larry Harvey, passed away in 2018. For all its attempts at inclusion, Burning Man in Black Rock City is a world that is mostly accessible to a privileged few with enough time to take a weeklong break from reality. And for all the gifting that takes place, it takes a lot of money to get out there.

The Regional Network's events make the experience more accessible to people around the world. Their smaller size takes us back to the basics, while adding a different cultural flavor to the social experiment. They offer new testing grounds for the principles of the movement, and how these apply 30 years on in a now-transformed and digitalized world. Regionals are held on every continent; one year visiting Burners even held their own mini Man Burn at McMurdo Station in Antarctica! A number of these are sanctioned events that meet standards established by the Burning Man Regional Network, and in 2019 there were 108 official Regional Events. Many more are unofficial events that still celebrate Burning Man culture and principles.

As Burning Man has grown from a gathering on Baker Beach to a worldwide community it seemed timely to explore the similarities and differences between participants at a Regional event and the larger Burn in Black Rock City (BRC). Maybe it is here that we can find the answers to the seeds of a global movement which has the potential to offer new models of living. The genius of Burning Man is that it provides a structure for the development of a non-structured community. In doing so it gives power to the participants to dream up their own city.

So with this intention I uprooted my life, mapped out a schedule where I would cover seven Burns across six continents within a year starting in Fuego Austral (April 2018 Argentina) before traveling to AfrikaBurn (May 2018 South Africa), Midburn (May 2018 Israel), Nowhere (July 2018 Spain), Burning Man (August 2018 US), Burning Japan (October 2018 Japan) and Blazing Swan (April 2019 Australia). I worked remotely throughout this time to self-fund the trip, or I could simply not have afforded it, so it was at times intense. I mostly traveled alone and many times out of my comfort zone. During each trip I would try to embed myself as much as possible with the local Burner culture, joining local camps and connecting to the various Regional organizers for their insights on what made their version of the Burn special.

The Burns were all vastly different, whether in a field of fewer than 500 people like in Argentina or Japan, or in the deserts of Israel or South Africa where more than 10,000 people come together to celebrate their local Burn each year. Each was a mirror of the culture, with different ways to approach community building, inclusion, art and self-expression, and varying degrees of raucous revelry. But ultimately it was the similarities that stuck the most.

Each Burn is a journey that teaches you something about yourself, building to a crescendo as the week accelerates. From the preparations, the first impressions and setup of a temporary city, to the fiery cathartic rituals that mark the end, solidifying the sense of collective experience, with every Burn, we remember that fire made us who we are as a people, and something deep within stirs.

Writing about the movement was a way to give back to the community that had inspired me. The more Burns I participated in, the more I felt compelled to spread the word about Burning Man's culture. I journaled each of the Burns I attended and found myself compelled to write about the sensations, sounds, textures and goosebump-worthy moments that stayed with me after each experience. To try and convey that sense of sensory immersion the Burn provides that puts you in flow state. Because in the end, there is no rational logic to why we are drawn back to an inhospitable dust bowl or to live in a tent in a field in the middle of nowhere. Quite simply, the magic that we can create when we are given a space to create, play, give and connect without limits knows no borders.

The essence of the Burn is the need for human connection and the ability to make that connection—both one-on-one and 80K-on-80K at the same time and in the same place. That longing to be part of something that's bigger than ourselves. Here we build creative "cities" where everyone is celebrated, temporary sanctuaries of connection. This personal account seeks to offer an insight into these micro-worlds, and provides reflections on the context in which they are created.

What started out as an idea to report on the culture would eventually turn into a five-year project, to which I would dedicate countless hours. But what I didn't fully realize at the start is how much it would change me on a personal level.

We all seek out our own version of a hero's journey at some juncture in life. The self-reflection that happens when you are on the road can be deep, and at times painful. The playas of the world are not just playgrounds for good times. They can also give you the type of experience and tough love that tears your guard down and cracks your heart open. And from here you have the opportunity to look inward and patch it back together.

Would it have been wiser to stay in the security of a stable job and city life rather than taking off? Probably. Would it have been easier to keep my demons at bay rather than having several existential crises miles away from home? Definitely. Was it worth it? A thousand times yes.

As the journey ended, a global pandemic took hold and tested the strength of our communities. The whole world was in turmoil and, like many around me, I faced one of my toughest years. Most major gatherings including Burning Man were paused. This only added more urgency to sharing what I had learnt in these temporary cities around the world, and how they transform us with their clarion call to the artist within. I invite you to open your heart and immerse yourself in a journey across six continents.

For millennia we have gathered around the fire—just like we now do at Burns around the world—to share stories. *Once Upon a Time in the Dust* is mine.

Chapter 1:
Fuego Austral

ARGENTINA — 28 MARCH - 2 APRIL 2018

*A*rriving in Argentina I felt the familiar thrill again, to be reunited with a family, with a community. A place that is filled with strangers, but that will soon feel like home. The format of Fuego Austral is vastly different from that of the Black Rock City event. That gigantic expanse of dust in the Nevada desert, the city that is built out of nowhere. 80,000 masterminds creating it in unison, an outpouring of creative energy and childlike wonder, full of playfulness, but also a demonstration of incredible skill and organization.

The Fuego playground is barely 500 people strong; how will it compare? I am full of curiosity and hope for the experience that lies ahead, with the Fuego Austral mantra *"la experiencia será lo que hagamos de ella"*—"the experience will be what we make of it"—firmly in mind. The simplicity and poignancy of this message encapsulates the very essence of what a Burn should be, and its Argentinian architects have created a channel for it to come to life in a way that takes us back to basics.

As I land in Buenos Aires, the Southern Hemisphere summer is starting to loosen its torrid grip, giving in to the soft temperate glow of autumn. The pace starts to slow and the humidity dips as nature prepares for its yearly slumber, the landscape turning varying shades of rust. The harshness of one of the coldest winters on record in Europe starts to fade into memory as I peel off the heavy layers of clothing that I've been mummified in for months.

Life is made up of a sequence of moments, and right now I am communing with myself as the journey that I've planned for so long finally comes into being. My pulse accelerates in the sweetest of ways as I walk out into the sunshine, letting it all sink in, feeling alive. It has been six months to the day that I decided to embark on a voyage to unearth what community means across the four corners of the globe, and what better place to take the first steps than South America?

The Latin American spirit has an uncanny way of lifting me up when I am down. The land vibrates with passion and soul. Out here the people seem more strongly connected to their emotional core. Perhaps this is due to building communities a million miles from home. Or maybe it is pooled in the energy of the indigenous blood that still flows like an estuary through the continent.

Further north from here a whole land filled with ancient teachings and spirituality lies in wait. Many are irrepressibly drawn to it, traveling to connect to those energies through shamanic rituals deep in its jungles, using plant medicines to unlock ancestral visions and open up pathways of light. As modernity numbs society with its dangerously lobotomizing form of capitalist and materialist anesthetic, a tribe is breaking away with arms outstretched to run madly towards feeling, connection, community and togetherness, deeply inhaling the present moment.

Buenos Aires rushes past us as we drive to its center, taking in the organized hustle and bustle of one of the most iconic Latin American cities. The city center develops outward from the *Plaza de Mayo*, its historic square. Sprawling boulevards, narrow shopping streets and outdoor cafés are laid out like a European metropolis, marked by a fusion of Spanish and Italian that speaks of its colonial past and polyglot present. It is a cosmopolitan city created by immigrants, a melting pot of different peoples.

In many parts of the west, past a certain age people seem to retreat to their homes, and it feels like the big cities largely cater to the under-40s, but here old and young are out and about, mixing and chatting on the street. Argentinian communities feel inclusive and families are often extensive, tempestuous, and tight-knit.

Verboseness is a feature of gatherings with family and friends, dinners extending for hours over *sobremesa*, or table-talk, long after the eating is done. In this warm and tactile culture men kiss on the cheek, and friends gather regularly around *asados*, or barbeques.

Later in the trip the Fuego Austral organizers would invite me to a customary *asado*. As the meat sizzled on the grill, they talked me through what motivated them to set up the event. After coming back from BRC in Nevada, they were surprised that there was no Regional on the continent given the strength of the community here.

What followed was a labor of love to actualize their dream, creating the first ever Latin American Regional Fuego Austral, or Southern Burn, event held in 2016. The following year Fuego was hit by massive rainfall and gale force winds that flooded the site. It looked more like a scene from Glastonbury festival in the UK than a Latin event, and the effigy was soaked through, too wet to be burnt. Still, participants took it in their stride putting their inflatable water floats—including a large pink flamingo—to good use, as one of the organizers explained with a laugh.

My host in Buenos Aires is a fellow Burner I met in BRC, Burning Man's home in Nevada. Though we met for a total of only three days out in the dust he is already like family. He comes along for the ride, and with typical Latin American hospitality, invites me to stay with him.

As evening falls on my first night, the town surges with life in the vibrant and crowded entertainment district. People don't head out until after midnight to dance or chatter loudly, pressed against bars. Time is relative here and "we'll be there around 10 p.m." translates to "not before 1 a.m." to the trained ear. Given my jet-lagged state I agree to go out for a couple of hours, and of course don't get home till dawn. Partying is firmly ingrained in Argentinian culture. Electronic music blares out of *boliches*, or nightclubs, lining the streets, heaving with a cool and edgy crowd.

The next morning is the Day of Remembrance for Truth and Justice, a public holiday in Argentina commemorating the victims of the Dirty War, a seven-year period of state terrorism in the 70s and 80s. I join the march that grinds the entire city center to a halt. The Porteños' attitude is tinged with fatalism and pessimism about the country's direction and economic problems. Repeated cycles of hyperinflation mean that youth live precariously, and need outlets to disconnect from the strains of daily life. Perhaps it is because of this that Fuego has a particular appeal.

This backdrop has created a proud, passionate, and outspoken people, seduced by beauty and vibrant with expression, who rally together and know the value of community. This spirit pours forth in giant murals splashing the walls of Boca with color, plays that fire up the Teatro Colon stage, and writing that makes the heart tremble. As I walk through the Recoleta Cemetery that houses the country's most celebrated heroes, or stare back at the stoic faces gracing the capital's museums, the charisma that these figures exude is undeniable.

The nation is locked in a tug of war of traditional values and modernity, a juxtaposition of landscapes, cultures and political games. It is mired by the unpredictable rise and fall of a fragile economy, and peppered by a potent mix of masculinity clashing with a growing, outspoken femininity. It's as if the very body of the capital moves with the drama of an unfolding tango, each movement pulsing with emotion. It is within this context that a social experiment of community called Fuego Austral will play out near the tiny town of Tandil. A week filled with artists and dreamers yearning to escape the intensity of the city to join together in creation.

We pile what will sustain us for the week into my host's grandmother's car, buzzing with anticipation as we embark on the five-hour journey. Fuego Austral takes place in the *pampa,* or grasslands. As the city fades from view the landscape turns verdant; lush pastures stretch out for hours in endless flat and fertile lowlands. We are in the home of the *gauchos*, migratory horsemen guarding cattle on the great plains of Argentina.

The people are blessed with great beauty packed into one gigantic country. Magnificent falls cascade from lofty heights to pummel the ground with water in the sweltering heat of the north. Glaciers rise stoically from the water in the icy south, while mountain ranges dramatically carve the western border. Given the vastness, every region has its own distinct identity. It is no wonder that people who want to disappear from the face of the earth can so easily vanish into the wilderness here.

The landscape of the great plains is unchanging and hypnotic. Herds of cattle graze contentedly, blissfully unaware that they form the backbone of the country's economy. The *pampa* offers insight into a simpler way of living, one that has been lost in our modern era, one that many yearn for. In some ways the rural way of life is close to Burning Man's principles.

Speaking to the Fuego Austral organizers after the event, they explain that before build week they were welcomed into the house of a *campesino* (rural farmer) who let them live with him free of charge while they set up the event. Tandil seems miles away from the glamor of the city, the pace infinitely slower and more welcoming.

We arrive at night. Once on site we see dim lights in the distance and exchange glances and nervous smiles. At the gates we are met by three eccentrically costumed Greeters whose arms reach out to welcome us. We know at that moment that we are back "home." Our new city is still being built around us as we pull in.

The look and feel is more intimate, like the event itself. The art is wooden, simple, yet as much energy and passion, if not more, has been put into crafting it than at larger Burns. The lights are less blinding, less imposing.

Every year the organizers put on events in the city for co-creators to gather and strengthen the community before traveling out to the site. Here I met the team working on the *Camp Arco Iris* logistics, one of the many camps that would be set up at Fuego. In the run-up to the event, they had spent many hours designing and constructing the camp they would gift, including a giant rainbow structure that would eventually burn.

In many ways the contrast with the sensory overload of Burning Man art is a reflection of the culture. Where the Nevada event is reminiscent of the US, striving to demonstrate its scale and power, at Fuego it is more understated, yet proud, expressive, and full of meaning.

The artists walk among us in this intimate gathering, and as the week goes on we will get to know them all by name. The Man stands proudly at around five meters tall. A simple wooden structure, its arms raised high in the Austral sky in the classic Burning Man pose. It is a labor of love; many arms gather together to heave it up to its standing position.

The temple juts out like a cactus flower beside the Man. Its wooden branches are still bare but will be covered in scrawled handwritten messages and handprints as the week progresses. One of the messages I would later read stuck with me in transmitting the family-like essence of the event: *"seamos lugares que invitan a quedarse"*—roughly translating to "let us create spaces that are inviting"—but which has a broader meaning as it can apply to people too.

Further afield an hourglass called *El Reloj Sin Tiempo—The Watch Without Time*—is a poetic reminder of time's irrelevance. Time is something that we have fabricated to structure our lives, to mark the fleeting moments. The outcome is that we constantly live in the future rather than the present, our minds running away from us to tomorrow, next week, next year. It brings even more sting to perceived failure; we set ourselves goals that we must achieve within an often unachievable timeframe.

But in this space that we call the Burn we disconnect from this concept. Time is meaningless, and whatever folly we imagine in the present instant sets the tone for the day. Grappling with time is universal, a concept captured by Argentinian writer Jorge Luis Borges in the short story "Aleph," which describes a point in space that contains all other spaces at once, presenting the idea of infinity.

Those who are truly immersed in the present own the world, connected to an optimal state of consciousness and harmony with their surroundings. *El Reloj Sin Tiempo* reminds us of this, to leave all structures to one side and simply exist. This message is one of the pillars of the Burn experience and it is beautifully represented here, tilted to one side, wonderful in its simplicity but with a timeless message.

In harmony with the local culture, a giant *mate* pot stands in the middle of the field. Light filters through igniting it like a golden chalice against the backdrop of the *pampa. Mate*, a bitter tea drunk out of a gourd, originally grown on the jungle floor where it was discovered, is integral to Argentinian culture. It speaks to gifting, creating community through the ritual act of sharing, and represents a doorway through which new connections are made.

We sit around in a circle while a gourd of *mate* is passed between hands as a token of friendship, each observing the custom, passing it back to the *cebador,* who takes on the task of preparing and serving it. Connection is achieved through looking at the person you are handing the gourd back to, and an intention is set when giving it to them. Everyone sips in turn from the same *bombilla*—the straw propped in the gourd.

Throughout Argentina people observe this ritual; groups pass it among themselves in the city parks and public spaces, and it is not unusual for strangers to share it if you happen to sit next to them. This simple ritual speaks volumes of how the people of this land build rapport and community with ease.

The indigenous people here tell the story of a farmer, Misiones "Guarani," who saved the life of a native woman threatened by a jaguar. The woman turned out to be the personification of the moon, and in gratitude she gave the man the magical *mate* plant that wakes sleepers, stimulates the lazy, and turns strangers into friends. As we headed to the event I had been given a detailed lesson in the art of the *mate* ritual, and would later be told off for getting the steps wrong.

The next day we sit around camp, and our neighbors come to greet us. Such a simple gesture, but one that we are desperately hungry for in our modern world, to connect with those around us. Everyone is all smiles, a balm for the soul. There is no set plan, just conversation and sharing a vision of the world. We are free souls, free spirits, playful and open to the experience.

This is what makes a Burn unique, but is replicated across Burning Man's Regional Network. It is the people who set the tone, who make the magic, not a structure set up to entertain. In this simple field we create the experience together, we are all part of something special, going back to our communal origins. We pass the *mate* around, laughing together, disconnected from the stresses and strains, no phones, no internet, no mad rush to take us away from this shared moment. We remember who we are.

In the cities we are defined by our jobs. The connections we have created through technology are increasingly a parody of human connection. We are one of the loneliest societies which has ever existed, desperately seeking social recovery. Here we can commune again, crowded around a campfire, rediscovering the world together; disconnecting to reconnect.

During the day, theme camps spring up around us like mushrooms. A giant rainbow is raised up by people in multi-colored costumes. A girl covered in bright body paint carrying a rainbow-colored umbrella greets us with a hug. In another camp we lie on giant pillows under a red dome. The center camp structure is a small dome of hand-woven straw, light entering it from all angles. Activities for the week are handwritten on a board, with talks on love and family, astral readings and theatrical performances on offer.

Clambering through the site, dodging the brambles which treacherously trip us up, we hear the whistle of *The Sonorous Tree*, a simple structure acting like a wind chime, catching the *pampa* air. Such interactive pieces awaken our natural curiosity, creating experiences that stay with us.

At dusk a procession is organized by one of the camps. It takes a few days of adaptation to fully immerse yourself in a Burn setting; this usually happens in the initial 24-48 hours when you witness something of such beauty or feel an emotion so strongly that it blindsides you, spinning the default world topsy-turvy and fully immersing you in the experience.

As we join the procession I look around as a stream of people dressed in varied attire and billowing costumes walk in unison up the grass slope.

The sun is setting on the *pampa,* and on the colorful art and camps set up by those we walk with. The electricity is contagious and sweeps over us like a crashing wave. We hold hands and hug strangers and become a clan readying ourselves for a ceremony of ecstatic light and music, a celebration of life. The purr of music pulses in the background, filling the air all around us. We are intoxicated by the moment, lost in a sea of smiles, contrasting so starkly with what we experience daily in cities inhabited by shadows of ourselves. We dance under the luminous W-shaped strobe lights of the *Pampa Warro* until our weary legs carry us back to the sanctuary of our tent.

The sun rises slowly and surely over the quiet field, warming the huddled tents dotted around it. Emerging from our humble home, the first glimpse I catch is of a painted kite flying in the sky at Camp *Barrilete,* or kite camp. The stillness means that I can hear its gentle flutter and sway as it catches the wind. Smoke and steam rise from small camp stoves where people gather in circles, chatting the morning away, wrapped tightly in blankets, hair still ruffled by the night's sleep. A passer-by waves and smiles. I think about how strange it is that if I crossed paths with this same person in the city, we would probably never have exchanged a word.

While most of our neighbors are Argentinian, many people have traveled from neighboring countries and further afield to experience the Austral rendition of a life where money has no place, and art is freely given not because of its value or scale but because of the emotional connection it creates. Unlike some of the other Regionals, people here have an ability to get back to basics effortlessly. There is less inclination to excess or show. What is palpable is the tightness of the community, the warmth of the Latin American soul permeating all interactions. Everyone participates to make our home special in their own way. The sun sets, and we once again dance the night away.

The next day, Glamor Camp is putting on a mass wedding and we are all invited, not to observe but to participate. It is our special day to celebrate love for each other and this new community we have created. It turns the concept and sanctity of marriage between two people on its head, making it a collective playful affair full of lightness. Before the celebrations kick off, a fashion show is staged. Everyone, regardless of their body shape, walks to raucous applause, whistles, and cheers, lifted up to idol status by the crowd. Appropriately dolled up, we then make our way to the wedding celebrations.

As we approach the chapel the faces around us are all smiles and laughs, visibly moved by the emotion of the moment. The chapel is made of white cloth, and circles of deep purple and blues in sacred geometric patterns adorn its peaks. A wave of iridescent fabrics and jewels reflects the setting sun and catches the cool air like the sails of a ship embarking on a voyage. We join the long line of hopefuls waiting to be wed.

On this day we are all loved and accompanied in life; couples who have been together for years declare their love for each other with tears in their eyes, groups of friends fall into each other's arms collectively wed, strangers embrace in a fit of giggles, and some marry themselves. It is all ok. There is no right or wrong when we are given the freedom to love as playfully as we like.

One of the Fuego Austral organizers eventually steps up for their turn to get married, his two-year-old child running excitedly ahead. The bride's eyes dance, her long pink braids crowned by a white headpiece covered in shells and topped by feathers. The groom stands gleaming in a red jacket with fur trim. Their faces soften as they passionately embrace and kiss. The joy is infectious.

Of all the Burns I would attend I made some of the strongest bonds out in this field—that would stand the test of time. The Brazilian I "married" that day is now one of my closest friends, and since attending Fuego Austral, I have reconnected with many of these souls in different parts of the world like we had never been separated.

After the high note of the wedding, the frequency of the event shifts. The following days move at a slower pace while the nights accelerate, whipping participants into a frenzy. Friendships have consolidated; we flow as one. *Asados* are being cooked *en masse* in true Argentinian style. We cook and offer food to passers-by from our modest campfire whilst others throw large carcasses on open fires for all to feast on. I relax under the shelter of the giant tree shading our camp with outstretched leafy arms. I meander over to spend some time in the public library stacked high with books, and pass the official post office where you can send postcards to the outside world for free.

After sitting cross-legged with a participant, talking for a while, I am given a simple gift of a walnut tied to a string. It would be many months later that I realized the walnut was not an empty shell. When I finally opened it, I discovered a necklace encased within the shell. Each gift, carefully constructed, contained one of the 10 Principles. Mine read "Immediacy." This is the Principle that speaks the most to me, because aren't all Principles canceled out if they are not able to apply in the present moment?

Two years later I would randomly find myself speaking to her husband (who I had never met before) at Burning Man in Black Rock City. At the time I had set up an art project on Regional Burns and gifted him one of the postcards painted by my father, recreating a photo of a Man Burn scene at Fuego Austral. As he took the card, he looked at me in disbelief, pointed to one of the silhouetted figures in the front right and said, "That's me right there." He would then pull out an identical walnut to the one given to me by his wife years earlier at Fuego Austral as a gift. Pure playa serendipity.

Gifting without expecting anything in return is too rare an act in our modern society. Growing up my older sister and I were joined at the hip. She would put on puppet shows and design hand-drawn magazines for me when she was eight years old. Every two weeks, she would secretly put the paper magazines in the letter box and pretend they had been delivered by the postman to my squeals of delight.

A year later, I inadvertently spotted her at the letter box and the real identity of the author was revealed. My five-year-old heart swelled at the beauty of this selfless act of gifting. I pretended not to know so the secret deliveries could continue, and they took on a much deeper value for me. Far beyond any ready-made trinkets, it is the hand-crafted gifts made with love that hold the most worth and create the strongest human connection.

The night of the Burn, the wind picks up and the temperature drops. This means that the Man Burn has to be postponed until the next day. The eccentricity reaches a crescendo as we enter the final day. We pass giraffes in leopard-print coats being interviewed by men in sumo suits representing sumo TV before a sumo fight breaks out live on air. Camp *Barrilete* is playing live music, the bull head mounted on one of its columns greeting people as they enter the fray.

Breaking away, we retreat to the tent where all manner of hilarity ensues. We spend hours in the rabbit hole laughing till we cry. Camp *Pampa Warro* lights up the cold night with its strobing lights, while DJs in ponchos spin tunes. The night is ridiculous, freeing and alive. The Argentinians dance and move like liquid fire in a way that seems like second nature to them.

In the midst of the madness I am invited to a tent for some non-PG fun. This comically happens to be near the discarded carcass of a cow, no doubt sacrificed to an *asado* years back. I ask whether I will suffer the same fate if I accept, and we all fall about laughing.

The following morning breaks in stillness. We find ourselves gathered around the Man waiting for its sacrifice. The intimate feel of the event means that the crowd is only 300 or so strong, a contrast with the thousands that gather in a wild cacophony of mayhem at the US Burn. Instead of myriad art cars with blaring sound systems, a circle of drummers sets the beat of the moment. They start to sing for its sacrifice: "*Que se queme el Hombre,*" ("Let the Man burn,") they chant. Our eyes are fixed on the infinite movement of the flames which change like the elements, shifting in the same patterns of moving water or air in shades of orange, yellow and red.

This will be the first Burn I will see this year, and as my eyes scan the crowd, I can't think of a better group to share the experience with. Just like each sunrise and sunset, no two fires are ever the same. As the singing grows louder the Man falls a little lower, sparks filling the sky. We are surrounded by people who Burn with passion, the collective emotion rising as the compass of our city is burnt to the ground. We will leave no trace of this city, the fire living only in the memories of those who lived it together.

Fire occupies a sacred space in the ceremonies of many ancient civilizations and tribes. Though most Argentinians are primarily of European descent, ceremonies and rituals are numerous and complex in South America, and deeply embedded in indigenous ways of life. They are powerful connectors, allowing us to strengthen bonds with our communities and the natural world, as well as to access higher states of consciousness. Each person connects with what they have lived this year and projects wishes for the future out to the universe. The act of setting intentions is of itself a bit irrational, but as humans we tend to overwhelmingly wish for good. When we do so collectively, we raise the frequency around us.

As we leave the site we reflect on how we have made this experience what it was, channeling the message of this year's Fuego Austral theme, "Regeneration Fractal." Like fractals, we are in constant movement and evolution, growing and reinventing ourselves like living cells. We move in never-ending patterns, ongoing feedback loops, mirrors of the dynamic systems that move around us in the natural world. This is our time for rebirth, bringing harmony to the regeneration of a world in flux. This is the challenge of our generation. We practice the revolution of social consciousness and must carry it with us out into the wider world.

Starting small was the perfect way to set the scene for the Burns that would follow from this Austral point on the west of the Southern Hemisphere to one of its most eastern coasts. This would be my first time at a Burn with fewer than 10,000 participants. Going to Fuego would be a defining moment experiencing the power of smaller Burns. It confirmed that our realities and the way we interact can shift even though the environment remains largely unchanged, far removed from the sensory overload that can be found at larger Burn events.

Although I have learnt to get out of my shell over the years, I naturally tend to seek out the closeness of smaller groups. Here, I was able to interact with people on a one-on-one level, without distractions from ever-present phones. The Argentine way of life felt different to my Anglo-Saxon upbringing, where emotions are kept buried deep, and the cold indifference of people I had experienced while living in London. Over time, my friendship group had all settled down and my last years living in the city had become increasingly lonely and uneventful. Entering this space made me realize just how hungry I was for human warmth and connection, and to unplug from the grid.

For the first two months of my journey, I took time off work to be able to fully immerse in the Burn culture. This would be the first time I would have more than a couple of consecutive weeks off in ten years. And even then following up on emails would get in the way. Time and space for reflection is so crucial to the human experience, yet we go through life in a constant state of action and distraction as it passes us by.

The insightful book *The Art and Science of Doing Nothing* highlights how in Confucian times idleness wasn't a subculture but an integral part of culture. Another passage goes on to say, "The brain seems to need things like freedom, long periods of idleness, positive emotions, low stress, randomness, noise, and a group of friends with tea in the garden." How true this had felt over a cup of *mate* out in the *pampa*. For the first time in a long time, I started to properly unwind and reconnect with others and myself.

Chapter 2:
AfrikaBurn

REPUBLIC OF SOUTH AFRICA –
23 - 29 APRIL 2018

*T*otally shattered from my awe-inspiring adventure through the Latin American Burn scene, I land in Cape Town. The city is breathtaking. Table Mountain rises dramatically and verdantly from the land and the Atlantic Ocean skirts its edges, swelling gorgeously with waves. Trees lining the coast are blown sideways by the often-brutal force of the Capetonian winds, digging their roots deeper, craning their weathered necks over the road at gravity-defying angles.

The young and beautiful congregate and mingle in slick seaside bars. But against this polished exterior, the poverty here is dire and the racial divisions striking. Against this backdrop, a desire for a social experiment has sprung up in the southernmost point of a continent, deep in the desert.

From its infancy in 2007 AfrikaBurn has become the second biggest Burn movement in the Regional family, growing steadily to 13,000 inhabitants. It is centered around 11 Principles. The same set of 10 Burning Man Principles apply, but with the addition of "Each One Teach One," to encourage the passing of knowledge between community members. It is a city in its own right, attracting a mainly white population from all over South Africa, but swelling with a growing influx of European attendees. Still the South African contingent is strong and mighty, giving it a flavor that sets it aside from other Burns, manifesting in its brazen party-hungry citizens and towering earth-colored wooden art.

AfrikaBurn is the first of the regionals I ever experienced and combines my love for the continent and the Burns. I have always felt a strong pull to Africa, and have spent my career working on social projects here. Perhaps this is due to my grandmother being Black Caribbean of West African descent. Or maybe it is a byproduct of a childhood spent with my head in the clouds and dreams of a just world. I have traveled to over 15 African countries and lived for extended periods in the Democratic Republic of Congo (DRC) and Zimbabwe. The media tends to portray the continent in a uniform way but its 54 nations are anything but. It is a continent rich in contrasts and wealth, and there is a closeness to its communities that is unequaled in the world.

South Africa is packed with natural beauty, and the wilderness like the one found in the Tankwa desert, where the event is held, is astounding. I even considered moving to the country permanently given its breathtaking landscapes and easy access to the wider region. Driving through its nature reserves is an unforgettable experience, and the meeting of the two oceans, Atlantic and Indian, that straddle its shores permeates the air with salts that create flora unique to the country. I often visit the legendary Kirstenbosch botanical gardens in Cape Town, getting deliciously lost in its scented avenues. In the warm autumn evenings, I meet Capetonian friends and we gather for *braais* or barbecues in the city before the event starts, while I take in their easy-on-the-ear South African accents.

But despite being a friendly and welcoming country, the societal divisions here run deep as a legacy of its troubled history. It is unsafe to be out at night in many parts of the big cities, and the wealthy tend to live in heavily gated communities. Given the injustices that still exist, perhaps it is the desire to create a more just social order that has driven AfrikaBurn's growth, which was started by liberal South Africans committed to social change—the activism culture here is very strong.

The event is located in one of the most marginalized parts of the country, and its organizers have established a number of year-round initiatives to support the local community. This includes a post-event "collexudus" which feeds the local school for the entire year, as well as the "Hammer School" set up by the Department for Public Works (DPW) AfrikaBurn equivalent which teaches basic skills in carpentry and welding. While the makeup of the event is predominantly white, the organization is taking steps to bridge this gap by providing heavily discounted tickets and access grants to facilitate transport to the Burn. Beyond barriers to entry, they are also committed to integrating new attendees, for instance, through a mentorship program for people coming from townships.

Though there is still some way to go to make it fully representative of the Rainbow Nation, the event is one that has a distinctly African flavor and offers a magic that floods the soul, as only an experience in the backcountry of the cradle of mankind truly can.

Given the relentless Burn schedule I have set for myself, the usual preparations are condensed into one manic afternoon of buying the array of survival provisions which will sustain us for the week. This was to be my third time at AfrikaBurn, so this was not a virgin journey for me.

In a haze of delirium, we board the bus which leaves at midnight to hit the infamous tire-shredding dirt track that leads to the event site. Cape Town, the Mother City, arguably the most orderly and sanitized in Africa, fades into the distance as we rumble towards the wildness of the Tankwa desert that we will call home for the next week.

The journey is long, bumpy and frankly makes for a sore backside, but we make our way to the gates at dawn against the backdrop of a trademark African sunrise. The giant orb rises steadily, sending its powerful rays darting across the arid landscape. Tankwa's characteristic shrubs are burnt gold by its light, lining the dirt track that leads to the gates of the ephemeral city. The temperature starts to soar along with our anticipation.

This year the theme is *Working Title*, representing the temporary name that is given to a project during its development. This is in stark contrast to the previous year's theme *Play*, which resonates well with the Burner spirit, inviting careless abandon and tomfoolery to accompany an event where creative light-hearted participation is the name of the game.

However, a Burn is not brought together without effort from its participants and it is this fact that's often crowded out by the otherworldly pictures of the event. They paint an idyllic and superficial picture of life on the desert, but are largely silent about the less sexy elbow grease that goes into erecting a city and community out of thin air as a place to live arm-in-arm for a week. This includes basic necessities like porta-potties for participants. It is worth taking a moment to appreciate the work that goes into the compost toilets at AfrikaBurn. They are roofless and open to the elements, offering the best overhead views of the African star-studded sky at night—a far more enjoyable moment than offered by their enclosed plastic cousins.

The organizers describe this year's theme as one that "invites you to engage with the level to which you are responsible for defining Tankwa Town, a temporary city in a participant-driven society." Engagement is a word that so aptly defines the social movement that is this Burn. Disengagement rules so much of our default worlds: disengagement from our communities, disengagement from the natural world, disengagement from ourselves. Here all of these worlds collide and give one a sense of reconnection that is so lacking in our daily lives. There is no dull tapping of the computer keys, or silent blinking in the disruptive glare of our phones. There is the realness of interaction with the natural elements, of being embraced by a multitude of kindred spirits, of finally listening to the stillness of one's inner voice.

Registration complete, the virgins amongst us dive to the ground and rise to their feet giggling and euphoric, covered in Tankwa dust, starkly different from the fine white sort of the Nevada *playa*, a term which there derives from the geologist's word for a dry lakebed, but which across the Regional world has come to signify any ground on which a Burn event takes place. Here it is earthy and coarse but no less sacred, and as we gaze across its vast and desolate plains, we imagine the land being walked by the peoples who were sustained by it for centuries.

The sound of the welcome bell still ringing in our ears, we go forth into the arid landscape, rocky underfoot. The African sun is harsh by this time. We haul our weary selves and belongings across the dusty stretch and start looking for our camp. All along the avenues that line Tankwa town, camps are setting up. They form the *buitekring*—outer circle in Afrikaans—where the citizens will build their makeshift homes for the week, while the *bin-nekring*—inner circle—is equivalent to the Esplanade in Black Rock City. Further afield, in what would be deep playa in BRC the night lights up with the thousand lights of roving art cars and revelers crossing the African desert.

I am camping with AfrikaBurn's Burners Without Borders (BWB) equivalent called Outreach. Although many regions participate in creating social programs in their year-round communities and there are many local BWB chapters, AfrikaBurn is notable in its focus on this area.

As a true exemplar of the Burn's "Radical Inclusion" principle, Outreach offers grants to artists from the local community looking to attend AfrikaBurn. The Spark Grants program was launched in 2017, offering microgrants for community-based projects. In 2018, eleven grants are awarded aimed at increasing diversity at the event, as well as urban and Tankwa upliftment. This includes organizing for a group of traveling circus performers to take part and perform in the city. We search for our camp for what seems like an eternity, and end up setting down our bags and putting up our tent in one of the neighboring camps for the evening, too excited by our first night in town to stand still.

The beauty of AfrikaBurn truly comes alive after sunset. Dusk in the African sky puts on quite a show, shades of pink and red colliding and the sun turning red and fierce. The Karoo desert is one of the best places on earth to see the Milky Way with the naked eye. The black night sky sparkles with a thousand stars turning and twisting into mesmerizing constellations. Shooting stars often cross its canvas at lightning speed before disappearing behind the dark outline of the distant mountain ranges. Gazing up at its enormity is a reminder that we are all part of the universe's magic. It is the mirror through which we glimpse the merging of the natural world and the mystic forces beyond, vast and timeless, containing so many untold wonders.

All around us a buzz is starting to emerge from every corner of the newly built town. The soft chatter of voices resonates through the night as old and new friends meet and greet. Everyone has a spring in their step and a lightness permeates the atmosphere.

We make a pit stop at the Alien Café, an AfrikaBurn institution, which serves up a vital playa beverage: hot coffee. Backlit LED alien faces act as beacons, saviors for lost souls trying to make their way back to camp. Many conversations will be had while propped on its inviting cushions with people appropriately dressed as if they are from another planet, like their alien hosts.

Within moments I spot friends from Zimbabwe and South Africa looking in their element. We set off together and I am introduced to a local Ranger who would become a major character in my Burnstory. Moments later, we part ways and, as is so common in this gloriously technology-free zone, we will only cross paths again by chance.

Clambering through the *binnerking*, we suddenly see the central effigy rising in the distance. The Man of AfrikaBurn is called the *San Clan*. It is a uniquely South African symbol, taken from San culture, the oldest inhabitants of Southern Africa. It stands a good 20 meters tall, with one body, several heads and dancing feet, and is based on an image from the Eastern Cape Province, where it's found in San drawings in the sandstone caves and rock overhangs. Legend has it that it represents the sensations of having extra limbs as a result of shamanic dancing performed during trance dance ceremonies of healing or rainmaking. The symbol speaks to release and ritual, so entrenched in African folklore and traditional communities the world over. The AfrikaBurn organizers sought the approval of Khoi/San elders for use of the image, and members of Khoikhoi and San elders participated in AfrikaBurn 2016.

It is a beautiful ode to the communities of afore that shaped this land into what it is today. Their spirits wander amongst us out in the desert, their presence gracing the stars above and deeply rumbling in the desert's earthy underbelly. The many legs of the *Clan* dance to different drums, just as is true of South African culture. The *Clan* speaks to us all.

Even though we may seem far removed from the rituals of our ancestors today, we still seek out celebration and dance, allowing us to release and connect with each other and ourselves in wild abandon. This is an absolute truth, though colored by our modern world of machines and bright lights, and nowhere is the frenzied abandon more visible than here, rising to a crescendo as the week unfolds and accelerates.

The next morning we set out looking for our camp, reciting the coordinates to every single person within a short radius before realizing it was meters away from where we had pitched our tent. We literally lift our tent and all its contents and set it down in its final resting place without even securing it, too impatient to continue our adventure.

Our camp setup this year is fairly simple with tents huddled together in a circle, and a firepit in its center for campmates to gather around and sing African choir songs. The effort that has gone into the camp is therefore primarily in terms of gathering this impressive troupe of local circus performers and getting them out to the Tankwa. Seeing how this social circus fit into AfrikaBurn and the ethos of Outreach's work particularly resonated with me, hence my rationale for choosing the camp.

This more functional setup contrasts with my first AfrikaBurn camp in 2016, where we built a 20 or so foot tall wooden platform topped by a giant ribbon-strewn dreamcatcher from which to see the sunset. This had required months of preparation and a joint effort by all campmates to erect at the start of the event, during particularly sweaty and draining afternoons of work. But seeing people clamber up the platform and dance as the sun set behind the perfectly aligned dreamcatcher made it all worth it. A few days into the event, and in an unforgettable moment of camaraderie, the whole camp gathered on the deck to celebrate a purple-themed wedding. One of our campmates, the designated master of ceremonies wearing long purple robes, symbolically sealed our union. We stood together in work and in play, joined in this space we had co-created.

Back to the present day's events, and adorning ourselves in our finery, we set out to explore. Time stands still in the desert; paths are crossed and connections are made ad hoc with no agenda, no commitment. On our journey we bump into an eccentric character with a map of Africa shaved into his chest hair. He wears a bandana on his head and his speech is slurred by the large joint hanging from the side of his mouth. We sit with him sheltered from the scorching sun under the cover of a shade structure. With his proud Africa chest map glistening, he recounts the story of the Tankwa people, pastoral herders who have inhabited the land for 2,000 years. We sit and listen, cross-legged like children.

The rest of the afternoon is spent running excitedly from camp to camp, exchanging stories and bellylaughs along the way. As the sun starts to make its daily descent something makes us stop and watch. A makeshift theater scene framed by fabrics of different shades of blue, from deep indigo to pastel and turquoise, billows in the cooling air, dramatically backlit by the setting sun.

Suddenly a breathtaking performance unfolds in front of us. Deep ocean sounds ring out in the desert and a crew of performers appear holding larger than life-sized iridescent fish puppets, gracefully parading in a synchronized and visually powerful dance. The puppets are made of recycled materials and bottles which gently catch and reflect the shimmering light of the setting sun. The performance is a beautiful reminder of the fragility of our marine environment, played out in a desert setting.

We sit down quietly and take in the wonder and weirdness of the scene. Behind the billowing curtains, the *Clan* stands in all its glory in the distance, arms stretched out towards the sky while powdery clouds hang in the air. The moment is overwhelming, filled with the magic that is so characteristic of the Burn. When human creativity and effort are played out in front of us in perfect harmony and synchronicity with the natural environment, where there are no distractions and we are able to blissfully surrender to the beauty of the here and now. Our hearts rise up in our throats as the soft ocean music rises and falls. As with all things in this whimsical land, the theme camp has a playful and cheeky side, and is aptly called The Wet Dream Aquarium. If this is the stuff of wet dreams, then sign me up.

Freshly brimming with emotion, we continue on our journey, making our way to giant multi-colored hammocks that we swing in effortlessly while the sky changes colors overhead. At night we join the dancing revelers. Thick electronic beats swell from the music camps that have sprung up overnight. Dressed in various costumes, thousands of feet pound the Tankwa in unison.

While the festival is African in its origin, the culture that binds Burns across the world is heavily permeated by the rave scene. Beyond its principles, one population the Burn attracts is a generation of youth that traditionally sits firmly outside the mainstream, left-leaning and undeniably privileged, with a taste for electronic music. These young idealists, who some might label as reprobates, are the pocket of society that generally shakes up an established order, seeking out ways to radically upgrade their lives, including through the inspiration that altered states provide.

Among the revelers is the Ranger we met the night before, in full swing in a white tutu, topless and shimmering in glitter, twirling a fairy-lit umbrella in a mad dance. For now, we merely sample the party, firm in the knowledge that we will return to it later in the week.

As we arrive back in our camp the previous scene is starkly contrasted. The African choir we are camping with as part of Outreach is gathered around the fire. Deep and steady, an African chorus rings out. Voices rise in harmony, each following its own path and frequency while at the same time intertwining and joining in a rhythmic melody. The drumbeats that accompany the voices ring out in earthy cords as the dust is pummeled on and off by the dark hardened hands that strike it, rising into the night like circular puffs of smoke. Some eyes are closed in rapture, to better channel the emotion in the voice pouring out like hot energy, electrifying us all.

Each note undeniably tells a story, heartfelt and tinged with melancholy of times past. As the song continues its tale, the voices intensify and the faces crease and contort dramatically against the blaze of the fire, which casts mystical shadows on those present. The scene is timeless, a group gathered around a fire, burning embers glowing bright, united in song, a reminder that music is the common thread that brings us together, cutting through boundaries to reach the soul.

As is customary here, the week's acceleration starts on Wednesday. We become accustomed to waking to a world where we rise every day with a hug. Such a simple act but one which is so sorely lacking in our modern cities. We go forth to the desert; as people ride by on bikes grinning from ear to ear, and costumes abound. An African woman wears a shimmery gold skirt which flutters in the wind, holding her circular straw hat in place, breasts proudly bared to the day.

The dust rises in the afternoon and we shelter from it in a bizarre museum celebrating the history of MOOP, or matter out of place (aka trash), at AfrikaBurn. That night we are invited to a party in a neighboring camp and dance till dawn. A traveling art car joins the party and its sound system blares out into the night.

The next day our campmates schedule an impromptu circus performance out in the desert. They are dressed in incredible costumes: giant green and blue geckos, multi-colored dragons, leotards and clown outfits with long colored stripy socks. The performers are all the shades of the Rainbow Nation. The colors of their outfits pop and their faces are painted with an African pattern, dots of white paint forming a semi-circle drawn around the eyes.

As the drums ring out, passers-by join the procession weaving through the city before stopping in a nearby camp. A circle forms around the troupe as they begin their acrobatic performance. Drummers warm up the crowd as the clapping and cheering grow louder. Clambering up on each other's shoulders to form human towers, they somersault and back-flip perilously through the air to the gasps of the audience.

The crowning moment is provided by the two-year-old daughter of two members of the troupe. A natural performer, she has been born into circus life. Dusty golden ringlets frame her cheeky mixed-race face as she works the limelight. As she is propelled and hoisted up into the air by the steady arms of her parents, she giggles merrily before clapping her hands and waving at the audience. Her giggle is infectious, and she oozes confidence and a lack of self-awareness that is especially pronounced in children, all too often drummed out in the formal schooling system.

The Burn brings together people from all walks of life, from circus performers to accountants, giving us all a place for play and radical self-expression, reminding us that there is no single right path in life. The Burn is a place where we can be free from judgment, where we can reconnect to the inner child.

Walking away from the scene we pass a magnificent white armadillo-shaped art car on our way to an Ethiopian tea tent. The tent is made of stretched red fabric dappled in sunlight, which makes for a warm atmosphere inside. The floors are carpeted in ethnic rugs and a live band plays in the far corner, a mix of flute, drums and rhythmic instruments. Large paper butterflies and stars hang from the ceiling. Somehow the people lying luxuriously around on cushions blend in perfectly, wearing flowing scarves and bell trousers in various exotic prints, and we sit for a while to soak up the atmosphere.

Evening time creeps in, and we have been invited to AfrikaBurn's famous Leopard Mafia party at Camp Now. Spirits are running high in our camp after the earlier performance and we all don leopard costumes. Our campmates paint our faces with the same African semi-circle of dots, and for that moment we feel accepted as part of their troupe.

During the week we have felt a growing rift with the camp; we have been treated with a mix of interest and suspicion as white foreigners. We are separated from our campmates by social and racial barriers, which makes communication difficult at times as the week progresses. This feeling of division is something that plays out all over South Africa, and it is also felt here. While our campmates were initially welcoming, it is clear that they are not fully letting their guard down.

It is far from surprising that this would be the case. After all, despite its guiding principles, as a participant-led event the Burn mirrors the culture that exists outside its gates. There is still much work to do to make AfrikaBurn more inclusive to all, including the black majority in South Africa which still only makes up a fraction of the population here despite the efforts of the organizers.

Given the backdrop of social tensions, we respect the distance and try to help out with camp chores where we can to bridge the gap. Still, for now we enjoy a moment of camaraderie with our campmates as we prepare for the leopard dance together. Dancing and celebration is a way to break down the social barriers that separate us. The frenzy is already well underway as we arrive at the party. The sun is setting lusciously in the distance and one of the partygoers has climbed on top of the sound decks to spread her giant wings and twirl in a mad dance.

After dancing our leopard fill, we venture out to explore. Making a pit stop at the Alien Café, we natter with a giant bunny, then stop by a desert tennis court. It is a sight that would be odd in the default world, but some-how makes total sense here: a large tennis court has been set up, illuminated at night by a single powerful strobe light and decked out with fairy lights, decorated with colorful bunting hanging overhead. A man with a large blond afro and fairy-lit headband makes a serve, missed on the other side by a man in a long beige dressing gown, who is immediately heckled. The ball is larger than life, perhaps five times the size of a normal tennis ball, and passers-by stand and watch the game while dancing to electronic music that blares from speakers overhead. Not your run of the mill Wimbledon match.

Onward we go into the night in search of the next vibe. To the dismay of many attendees, some of the major sound camps have not made an appear-ance this year, specifically Skaduwee and the Spirit Train. Their absence is felt out in the African desert, and the beats that ring out from the camps are a bit too overpowering. A large South African contingent has decided not to join

AfrikaBurn this year because of this very fact. To put it into Black Rock City context, the Spirit Train is what the Mayan Warrior art-and-sound vehicle is to the Nevada playa while Skaduwee would be akin to Opulent Temple. We stumble for kilometers through the quarry that is the Tankwa desert to a disappointing music selection.

My mind casts back to my first year at AfrikaBurn. I imagine for a moment that the Spirit Train had suddenly pulled into the station; deep tribal beats filling the Tankwa sky and shaking the earth underfoot as the train rumbled into view, irresistibly beckoning all those it passed to join the ride. In an almost "Thriller"-like choreography, a hundred people broke away to partake in the mobile rave, letting out a deep battle cry in unison as they did. I ran with them following the tribe, giddy with excitement. The Spirit Train is an impressive mobile art train and its insignia, and arguably spirit, is *el lobo*—the wolf. It weaves through the desert forever growing its pack, to music that makes the soul howl. Its presence was sorely missed this year.

Friday is upon us and time is running out. The camp situation is growing more tenuous by the day and my mattress is deflating by the minute, moving like a tidal tsunami wave while I sleep, and tinned food is becoming increasingly unpalatable.

I return to the Ethiopian tea tent and a ritual of different teas. The tea master, an impossible eccentric straight out of an Aldous Huxley book, announces each blend as a beautiful girl in a golden brassiere with long hanging tassels pours it skilfully from a high angle into dainty cups. Milky, aromatic chais and deep herbal notes sweeten my grateful palate.

After this soothing respite from camp, I venture out with campmates to spend the day exploring art before the burns turn it all to ash. Plush art cars nonchalantly drive past, decked out in furs and sails. This sight would surely draw a crowd and hundreds of flashing mobile phones in the default world.

The art at AfrikaBurn is earthy, the structures are mostly wooden, almost makeshift, with an undeniably African flavor, and as practical and amusing as they are majestic. An art piece made of sticks jutting out to the sky with what look like circular bird nests attached to its ends appears in front of us, a hammock-like netting tied underneath for people to rest in. Another wooden shrine with people clambering all over it has a warning sign that says, "Feels unsafe? Maybe it is!"

Slowly under the heat of the Tankwa sun, we approach the temple which stands opposite the *San Clan*. It is called the *Temple of Gratitude*, designed by its creators to provide a space for us to acknowledge all that we are thankful for. It is inspired by the Celtic Father-Daughter Knot which, legend has it, was knotted by a girl on her father's deathbed, to say thank you for everything he had done for her. The design of the arches, the floor and the entrances are all based on this knot. It is much smaller in size than the *Clan* and has a palm leaf roof, reminiscent of a traditional African hut.

At night the temple is illuminated in red, and the shape of its archways diminishing in size as one walks towards its center are undeniably reminiscent of a vagina. It is not the great megastructure of the temple that we know at Burning Man, which offers an elaborate place to grieve and let go of our loved ones, but a simple shrine reminding us to express gratitude in life, to be happy with what we have. Its small size and simple structure point to an appreciation for the little things, as if to remind us that the humble man is often the most content.

As I reflect on this in a moment of introspection which the temples of the Burning Man world tend to inspire, I spot an inscription on one of the arches against the backdrop of the *Clan*. It reads, "If everyday life was like the Burn—we would all be freed!" This message is one I keep close in my default life. Its simplicity lets one assign any meaning to it. To whoever wrote this, thank you; it rang as true that day as it rings now.

Heading back to the *binnekring* we pass by a fashion show. Dusty Burners walk up and down the makeshift catwalk. This is not the fashion show you might expect at the Nevada Burn, where no doubt, highly preened

Instagram models would try and grab the limelight, tottering on tall platform boots. No, here the natural is favored, and the models are all the more beautiful for it.

A pretty girl carrying a red umbrella with her hair in braids, a virile looking man dressed in leather and wielding a large hammer; but there are also more outlandish contestants, like a dark-mustached participant in a green tinkerbell dress and bright yellow wig in braids. All flounce their stuff to the sound of the stagemaster who introduces them in hilarious fashion. Ahhhhh, the Burn! As the sun begins to set, a springbok parade dances past us, and a beautiful art piece with a map of Africa ablaze in its center makes us stop and watch.

The sunset is particularly mesmerizing today, and we sit ceremoniously, hypnotized by its graceful dip. All around, the vast and desolate Karoo stretches to infinity like an oil painting, towering mountains in the distance sketched out, shrubs jutting out from the hardened cracked earth.

There is no fence at AfrikaBurn, and attendees can wander out into the African wilderness for miles as they please. There is a tale of someone who did just that, disappearing from the world for two weeks and walking all the way to Cape Town, stopping in remote villages along the way.

The landscape here is majestic, the desert not as temperamental as its Nevada cousin. There is a timelessness and a stillness, a gentle swaying and crackling emanating from the vegetation when the wind rises up and whistles through its dry branches. The scorched earth has been kissed by a thousand sunsets, like a warrior bending to the ground in reverence, while it blushes a deep red. The sun sets abruptly here and the darkness and all the lights of the cosmos are wheeled in like a stage backdrop on cue, to steal the show.

Walking out a short distance from the lights and sounds of the city, it is obvious why the Karoo is one of the chosen places on earth for the Square Kilometer Array (SKA), a project to build the world's largest radio telescope to explore the universe. The SKA addresses "fundamental questions about the universe, the role of magnetism in the cosmos, the nature of gravity and the search for life beyond Earth." Thus, the Karoo is the site of one of the largest telescopes on the planet.

Looking up at the sky one can feel the pull of space; the stars shine brighter here, their cosmic patterns clearer, their secrets whispered just a little louder. The energy emanating from the universe is palpable, its teachings etched in the constellations overhead. I feel a deep sense of peace gazing up at its vastness. Once we quieten the chatter inside, we are at one with the wilderness. The African night sounds come into high definition, interspersed with the shrill clicks of the crickets. Bathed and radiating in moonlight, we reconnect and remember we are nature's children.

This is the night of the *Clan* Burn. There is a sadness as we approach the end of a long week, but also a pride at having survived it together, at having given this temporal city our all. We are invited into a warm camp for a night of indulgence, complete with bubbles and a warm meal, bliss in this harsh and arid land. Our matted hair and dusty fingers crack with dryness, and our water supplies are all but gone.

Come nightfall, crowds gather to watch sculptures being set alight; both the *Clan* and the Temple will burn tonight. As the fiery spectacles begin we sit silently together in the darkness. The *Clan* represents unity and community. The fire rises slowly, then engulfs the effigy in flames, burning down barriers which separate us in the default world. In the final moments the *Clan* twists its body while dramatically falling to the ground as if possessed in a final ecstatic dance, its many limbs surrendering to the throes of a week-long shamanic trance-like state. All around us, cheers and howls of wild abandon pierce the night as it crashes mightily into the embers.

Now the party begins in earnest. The *Clan* lives in all of us tonight. In every corner of the city bodies writhe on the dancefloor, beats pumping out breathlessly, passing through its desert children like electricity. We sway in unison under the lotus moon, hopping from stage to stage, sampling all the electronic beats alluringly on the menu. On and on the ecstatic dancing continues, furs are dramatically thrown aside, the brightest, most luminous, outrageous costumes saved for the best night revealed. Everyone is gorgeous and decadent.

The dusty who have been here for the week mix with the shiny newcomers gracing the desert with their presence for the weekend. All will give it their all tonight. We meet our Ranger friend, who's whipped into a frenzy, torso glistening with sweat and glitter, wheeling a mobile sound system around. Everywhere is a relentless need for one last night of wild-eyed freedom and fabulousness before the inevitable retreat to the sterility of our everyday lives. One of our newfound friends wields a luminous staff complete with an animal skull he found while climbing up one of the distant Tankwa hills. He dances with it as if possessed. Incredible.

Finally breaking away from this madness, we find a spot by a campfire where we can chat and recuperate from the frenzy. The temperature has plummeted, and we sit in our furs warming ourselves by the blaze. As is fitting we await the sunrise, which we have not seen since our arrival in the Karoo, to close the circle.

Together, we clamber up one of the remaining tall structures, a giant wooden nest that provides a perfect platform to watch the orb rising. We huddle closely with the twenty or so people who are already on the platform. Though we have never met we have lived through a week of shared adventures, and from this premise comes a shared bond. All smile warmly as we walk up and are invited to sit with them. They are not strangers.

The experience of shared humanity binds us together. As social creatures, we crave closeness and community. Yet our modern societies have taught us to put up walls and fences to separate and alienate ourselves from each other as our *de facto* mode of existence. But in this parallel world we have created, we are joined by the principles we have lived by all week, in a world of possibility where the only currency to have changed hands has been gifts. Huddled and shivering on the nest-like structure as the night draws to a close we feel alive, and with a renewed sense of hope. On this day in the African desert wilderness, together we look up at the new dawn.

As we pack up for the event and leave, disheveled and spent, with matted hair, we learn that Burning Man's legendary mastermind and co-founder Larry Harvey passed away the previous night, coinciding poignantly with Burn night at AfrikaBurn. Here in the cradle of mankind, we celebrated his passing through fire in a way that we hoped would fit the legend of the man.

The event had gone by in a flash. As it drew to a close, I was already too busy planning for the next installment of my journey to Midburn in Israel (taking place two weeks later) to fully process it. Beyond the festivities of AfrikaBurn and the incredible beauty of the Tankwa, what stayed with me was the interaction between my campmates at Outreach.

Despite the rift, I formed a bond with one of the younger members and we stayed in touch after the event. Later on, he shared stories of the challenges of life living on the fringes of a divided society. He conveyed to me that ultimately he was grateful for his experience at AfrikaBurn. It had given him some insight into communal living with a section of society that he would normally have little interaction with.

Even though AfrikaBurn includes the principle of radical inclusion, it is difficult to strip away the layers of our conditioning. As I have acutely felt many times as an aid worker, it is hard to shake off the divisions of our privilege and tear down the barriers that separate us as humans. The African philosophy of *Ubuntu*, which can be translated as "I am because we are," underpins the concept of an open society. In an interview Nelson Mandela explained the essence of this concept simply "during the old days a traveler would stop at a village and [he] didn't have to ask for food or water. Once [he] stops, the people give him food, entertain him." He goes on to say, "Ubuntu does not mean that people should not address [their own issues] but are you going to do so in order to enable the community around you?"

So many times I have asked myself why we cannot live more aligned to this philosophy, but struggled with the mental dilemma that I am on the comfortable side of the fence. We long for simpler ways of life but are shackled by the golden cages of our commodified existences.

On a trip to Kinshasa, the capital of the Democratic Republic of Congo, I saw sprawling shanty towns filled with people living in poverty. But once I left the city for the surrounding rural areas, and despite being equally materially poor, the people seemed to have a better quality of life. Here, they had retained a sense of dignity, living off the land in village communities.

When I took off for my year across the Regionals, one of my goals was to downsize my life. I gave away more than half of my possessions to charity before leaving London in search of a more nomadic existence. To this day I joke that my most permanent address is my storage space where I keep a couple of suitcases. But my memory bank is full to the brim. We can all do more with less. A traveling social circus troupe and a pared down existence in the wilderness of the Tankwa has much to teach us in this respect.

Chapter 3:
Midburn

ISRAEL – 14-19 MAY 2018

*O*nward to Israel with barely a week's respite. En route, I open my dust-covered laptop ready to let the feelings I have lived during the previous week at AfrikaBurn flow into words. Still flying high, I am in tune with the emotions warming my heart as the Middle Eastern dust beckons, soon to nurture my soul. Midburn, the Israeli Regional event, is named using two words: "*midbar*," the Hebrew word for desert, melded with "burn." This is the part of the journey I am the most unsure about. I cannot imagine what the event will offer, having no real connection to this culture. I didn't know then that the memories it would provide frame some of the most beautiful days and connections of my life.

A dizzying array of smells hangs in the air of Jerusalem's old town; the scent of millennia-old labyrinthine markets swarming with life in a way that seems chaotic to outsiders, but is navigated effortlessly by locals. The clash of cultures and religions comes to life; Jerusalem is the capital city of two peoples, and home to the temples of three religions. Centuries of pilgrims' feet have trod these streets, their owners jostling to honor their beliefs. The tension in the air is palpable, unlike anything I've ever experienced. Here everyone's mission is more important, each belief stronger than another's. And today, every sacred site is a photo opportunity. Temple Mount, perhaps the holiest site in the world, located in the Old City of Jerusalem, is of critical significance to Jews, Muslims and Christians alike.

Israel is small in size, but the history and natural jewels tightly packed within its borders are astounding. Israel teems with mountains and deserts, the lowest and saltiest of seas, holy citadels and paved alleys, and is criss-crossed by desolate winding roads as well as modern boulevards. Streets that Jesus walked still exist here. Jerusalem is a city of great beauty, described in the feminine in sacred Jewish literature. It is the birthplace of some of humanity's oldest stories, interpreted in ways that have given whole peoples their identity, and recounted kneeling in front of crosses, lighting menorahs, and crouched low on carpets.

That same afternoon I visit the West Bank. The territory is so named as it sits along the West Bank of the Jordan river, holding a Palestinian refugee camp along with scattered Israeli and Palestinian settlements. My eyes scan messages and graffiti on the West Bank barrier of giant concrete slabs. This concrete wall has now become an art mural covered in messages, including from the legendary street artist Banksy. It symbolizes the duality of life in Jerusalem.

Later I would visit Yad Vashem, the Holocaust remembrance center, which takes us through the darkest hour of the Jewish people. Emerging at the end of a tunnel, the rolling hills of Jerusalem open in front of us through a prism-shaped frame, the sun setting in its center. It is a powerful message of light after darkness. In some ways the Israeli people hold the key to showing the world a full cycle of healing. I wondered how the Burning Man Principles would manifest in this land. What is clear in this environment is that people need an outlet like the one provided by the Burn for release and self-expression.

I delay my journey to Midburn to take a trip to the Dead Sea, as I fear I may die from exhaustion and delirium having come from AfrikaBurn only the week before. Nestled in the Jordan Rift Valley like a shimmering blue diamond, it is the earth's lowest elevation on land. The journey is through hardened terrain, with every contested parcel telling a story.

In the sea I wade and float effortlessly in the hypersaline waters, shutting out the sounds of the world for a while, letting its therapeutic properties wash over body and mind. The sapphire water is so thick and dense with salt it feels almost oily. Later I bake in the afternoon sun while the dried salt pulls at my skin, the loud background chatter of throngs of tourists emerging from the sea comically caked in mud.

Keen to experience the stuff of Israeli legend firsthand, I journey to a kibbutz carved into a mountain and surrounded by a stunning botanical garden in the jaw-dropping nature reserve of Ein Gedi. The gardens of Ein Gedi are immaculately kept, pristine; each tall tree has a placard indicating the year it was planted, and the dates go back decades. The idyllic feel of the place cannot be overstated. Young people play and laugh together, living communally on the land.

In some ways, the tenets of the movement resemble the 10 Burning Man Principles, with communal effort at the core. It is no wonder therefore that Midburn has taken hold here at a dizzying speed; in a few short years it has grown to be the second largest Burn event outside the US, second only to AfrikaBurn. Quite a feat considering the difference in population: South Africa's population is 50 times that of Israel's.

I make the final leg of my journey from Jerusalem to Tel Aviv, and the difference is striking, not unlike journeying to a different continent altogether: a seismic clash of tradition and modernity within 40 minute's drive. Personalities in Tel Aviv are strong. Men and women walk the streets with self-confident chutzpah, heads high and gazes steady, faces turned firmly towards the future, not the past.

In this bustling Mediterranean town hugged by a fabulous coastline, everyone is out and about on the sun-soaked streets. Gorgeous bodies line the seafront, and the omnipresent sound of *matkot*, or Israeli paddleboard, on the beach is almost deafening on this hot summer day. Young men mill around on electric scooters, their pretty girlfriends pressed up against them in summer dresses or tight jeans. The city is progressive, cool and edgy, and the smells of marijuana and freshly ground coffee waft from the cafés.

Having spent the previous night unwisely downing shots in the holy city in a most unholy fashion, I arrive in Tel Aviv with a splitting headache. I meet up with the finest of newfound friends offering a ride from Tel Aviv to Midburn. Within an hour of meeting we have bonded and are dashing in a mad rush, buying all sorts of ridiculous Burn attire. We pile all of our gear into the car before crashing out to sleep but barely get any rest, overstimulated by the day's events.

It is in this state, in a car packed full of random crap and people, that I journey to Midburn with the experiences of my week in Israel replaying in my mind. Arriving at the event is somewhat anticlimactic. Unlike the marathon journey to most Burns, the Midburn site is just two hours from Tel Aviv and close to civilization. All around, camps are springing up like a military operation. Camp teams are highly organized and structured, having spent the best part of the year setting up fundraising events for their camps. The years of military training most participants have invariably been through means the event runs like a well-oiled machine.

I am staying with the famous circus camp, Cirque du Shlapy, something I have been particularly looking forward to. As I arrive already drenched in sweat from hauling my bags across the desert, I am greeted by performers of all sorts stretching and bending on the circus scaffolding, swinging from ropes and hoops. The sense of community in the camp is strong. Each member has a defined role, a purpose and place in the hierarchy. There is a food rota in place, with campmates taking turns to cook meals for the rest of the camp.

The infrastructure that has been painstakingly set up by the campmates is a true feat of teamwork. Our new home has a well-stocked kitchen area complete with wood oven and a shower, rows of orderly tents, a camp portaloo, and a colorfully decorated communal area with plush beanbags and cushions. Night and day when compared to my two previous rather basic camping experiences at Fuego Austral and AfrikaBurn.

It is searingly hot and dusty here in the most western point of Asia where East meets West. Walking through the desert and exploring our surroundings is like being transported to a biblical scene. This is the cradle of civilization, the ground itself heavy with the weight of battles between ancient tribes. The terrain ebbs and flows in golden sand and dusty ravines that we will spend the week exploring.

The art installations add further drama to the scene. The crowning piece is meticulously crafted: a majestic camel of intricately woven wood, rising up proudly under the midday sun. Head held high, its snout touches the desert sky, turquoise gems adorning its neck and underbelly with feathered wings made from desert palms.

The effigy stands beside it. Its design is based on the poignant story of "The Steadfast Tin Soldier," a fairy tale by Hans Christian Andersen about a tin soldier's love for a paper ballerina. The tin soldier stands on a single leg because, as he was the last one cast, there was not enough metal to make him whole. He sees a ballerina standing on one leg dancing and, recognizing himself in her, he falls in love. They eventually end up burning in a fire together, the soldier melting into a tin heart next to the ballerina's spangle which has turned black.

The representation of a soldier in an Israeli Burn is a figure that most can relate to given the compulsory military service. On a conceptual level, the soldier embodies strength and rigidity pitted against the litheness of the ballerina, a symbol of carefree self-expression. He is built as a square structure, whilst the ballerina is a slender curved pole with wooden arms shaped like a harp raised to the sky. She spins continuously on a platform with full freedom of movement, whilst he stands stoic and static against the desert landscape. They watch each other in this motion standing side by side. As she spins so the scene of the lovers morphs and changes in composition. The arc formed by the ballerina at times looks like a bow drawn by the soldier, metaphorically poised to shoot the arrow of love.

What the square is missing is roundness, something that is soft, gentle like the ballerina. The bottom part of the square soldier is hollowed out and rounded on one side so he appears to be standing on one leg observing her spin. During the day, light filters through the rounded part of the structure as if celebrating this softness. The central part of the soldier is left exposed, containing a red heart that beats like a beacon through the night.

Like the soldier, we all long for softness in a world that demands us to be hard, to be rigid. In this rigidity we stand incomplete, until one day we find the softness we seek in another—which in turn shines a light on our own. It strikes a chord deep within, and suddenly what we saw as our weakness becomes our strength. Only then can we find the balance to dance, the missing piece that allows us to shine with a full and beating heart. At the end of the week, the two structures would burn together symbolizing the union of strength and fragility, masculinity and femininity, stillness and movement. A striking and moving message in a land where hardness too often prevails.

Further afield the Midburn version of the temple also has a different symbolism from that of the Black Rock City structure of the same name. This year the organizers decided to try something different, creating a secular space that could be neutral and inclusive.

The Compass is not built as a shrine for grieving, but as a compass, symbolizes the finding of your path. Its message is one of journey and self-discovery. In the Jewish tradition temples or shrines have no place in the grieving process. Instead, a structured framework is provided to channel and express grief in times of loss. Unlike in my own culture, it does not unfairly ask grievers to put on a brave face. It recognises and gives space for the grief process to run its course, in some respects insular but always surrounded by loved ones. The burning of the temple as a grieving place could also be culturally discordant in that it suggests cremation, and Judaism stresses burial in the earth.

Another decidedly Israeli trait is razor-sharp humor. One can stumble across all manner of hilarious and interactive art installations in deep playa. One of these is a long circular plastic chute crowned by a portaloo. Participants can climb a ladder to the top, sit on their throne and very literally shit on the Ten Principles inscribed at the end of the chute below. A true masterpiece of self-derision. A camp offers "medical remedies" involving a "doctor" dunking peoples' heads in ice cold water before giving the unsuspecting participant a slap across the face as they emerge. Engaging in any form of banter often provides the most satisfactory of outcomes.

The randiness of men is also on a whole other level here. One of my camp members personifies this more than anyone. This man is built of muscle, short and compact with a frame like forged steel. His laugh can make just about anything sound suggestive. I casually ask him to hand me a bottle of water to which he replies, "You want water eh? Huhuhur." He spends his days flexing, gyrating, and air boxing.

Despite the seeming openness of Tel Aviv and the half-clad bodies that walk its streets, there is state security surveillance here at Midburn and restrictions are placed on nudity. It is the only Burn edition where you cannot walk openly naked or even with bare breasts. It seems the event almost didn't take place here due to government concerns about security and moral issues such as nudity. And yet the outfits here are far from demure; as long as parts such as offending nipples are covered, participants get away with being almost bare. Plenty of naked people can be found in Midburn's shower or "body cleansing" Camp Shtifale however, and it is fine to be naked in one's own camp as long as it's not out in the open playa.

Given how common nudity is across the different Regional events as a symbol of liberation, a celebration of the body away from judgment and the constraints of society, the concept of security guards patrolling the desert in search of a rogue nipple contrasts with the broader Burner culture.

Despite the nipple police in town, the usual tomfoolery appears unabated, and the Israelis, like our macho campmate, seem to thrive on good sexual innuendo. After this first recon I head back to camp where there seems to be no dinner tonight, so I snack on nuts in my tent, unaware that this would be the first day of a three day fast as those in charge of cooking were having a little too much fun at the event to observe the food rota.

The next day is spent exploring and sheltering from the stifling heat. The sun of the Negev desert pummels us relentlessly and temperatures build to a crescendo over the week.

I pass a giant pirate ship in the desert, its sails high. A miniature inflatable parrot flies comically tied to its mast. Techno blasts out of its speakers and a kaleidoscope of participants dance theatrically in front of it. One is wearing oversized flapping red wings that fly and twist like giant crab claws, another wears a giant technicolor hat. Parasols are twirled and pulse to the beat overhead, and water spritzers form little clouds of mist all around.

Midburn is good at desert ships. A couple of years ago artists recreated Noah's Ark docked in the sand, complete with recorded animal sounds inside the main deck. In the legend, Noah's three-deck ark reflected the three parts of the universe imagined by ancient Israelites: heaven, the earth and the underworld. The three definitely converge here: a utopic heavenly freedom and spiritual liberation, the aridness of the earth covering us head to toe and demanding respect, and the darker underworld emerging after nightfall.

Later I scale the dunes in darkness, lit by a plethora of LED lights, and meet some of my campmates for the first time. As with most of the Burns I've attended this year I have come to Midburn on my own, making connections along the way. In choosing which camp I would stay in, I thought how wonderfully outlandish it would be to finally run away and join the circus at least for a week, in a totally alien place where I did not speak a word of the local language.

Before arriving, I was apprehensive and excited in equal parts. Would I fit in? Would I be able to communicate? Would I feel lonely? All the questions one asks before venturing into the unknown and pushing boundaries, even just a little. When we push a little we get so much more out of living. I could not have wished for a better group to share my Midburn experience with. Theatrically minded outliers, nerves and bodies of steel, biting humor, and soft plush hearts that love a thrill.

Our nightly adventures take us to a tunnel hiding behind a heavy curtain. Turning our backs to the darkness we push the curtain back and enter a powerfully lit vortex of lights reflected in mirrors lining its walls. The installation is whimsical and without any obvious purpose but it strikes a chord in my soul that speaks to my inner child. This Narnia-like tunnel provides a portal to a magical mystery world behind a curtain.

The mirrors reflect the wonder in our faces. We close our eyes, and when we open them again the lights have diffracted into heart shapes bouncing off the surfaces. Big smiles. It is not just the scene which has transformed into a land of hearts, but our very hearts that have swelled and transformed with emotion.

The art and experiences offered at Midburn provide an immersive experience that can change one's way of looking at the world, peeling back the stale and grown-up layers to reignite the lighthearted awe within. The bonds that form when we are allowed to play together and create memories of shared joy seem indestructible.

That night the camp is in full performance mode. The bonkers master of ceremonies riles up the circus tent. With effortless grace a petite blonde acrobat hoists herself up on a hanging hoop, coiling her body around it like a snake before unraveling, legs outstretched in aerial grace, head thrown back to the rapture of the crowd.

A campmate with a chiseled physique, bare-chested with legs clad in shiny lycra, steps up next. He climbs the silks confidently to the ceiling, wrapping them around his body on his ascent. He hangs suspended for a moment then spins to the ground in a series of gravity-defying moves in perfect synchronicity, mastering each movement and muscle. Precision crafted from years of discipline.

My body is all chills watching this performance. Here is an artist in his element expressing himself to the fullest in this moment, totally at one with the flow. It is a wonderful and hypnotic gift. All around, crowds of people have gathered to watch the scene, sitting cross legged, eyes glinting in the dark.

Wednesday morning dawns, and my stomach growls like a beast. At this point I am absolutely ravenous, surviving on snacks and nuts I traveled with, but not having eaten a proper meal since arriving. The harsh desert environment has a way of opening up one's appetite. And then a miracle occurs.

Crouched in my tent like a rabid animal, a scent of food so delicious it brings tears to my eyes fills the air. I approach the camp kitchen where my campmates are making some form of mouth-watering *shakshuka*. I wait with bated breath for my plate to be filled.

Finally, a chunky tomato sauce with thick cut caramelized onions and chicken liver falls lusciously on my plate, and I am handed a hot pita fresh from the oven. Scanning the camp mess for a quiet corner in which to devour this platter of nearly unholy deliciousness, I decide to stand rather than sit so as to avoid small talk getting in the way of enjoying each morsel. As the first juicy bite floods my palate it is too much, nearly a religious experience. I wolf instead of savor, barely catching my breath in pure ecstasy.

Finally satiated, I fall heavily on the camp cushions and talk for hours with a stranger over coffee about life, disappointment, and the loss and find-ing of wonder. We share stories and smiles, but we do not talk about anything profound or life changing. By being here and able to connect, by taking our time without watching the clock with no hurry or stress, no agenda, we feel the warmth and comfort of a human exchange.

Our stories remind us of our shared existence, regardless of where we are from. We recognise a kindred spirit through a thousand non-verbal actions. The movement of the eyes, the way the brow rises and falls, the crease and curl of the lip. The frenetic pace of modern life means we lose myriad possible connections. In a vacuum of interaction, we lose our oneness with others and the wider world. Little by little this erodes our humanity. By creating a space where we seek out rather than avoid contact we can benefit immeasurably.

After this laid back morning I prepare for a momentous occasion, the Midburn wedding of two of our most beloved campmates. Dressed in our finest, the wedding party takes off in a sea of bejeweled smiling faces, white feathers, unicorn horns, and fabrics fluttering in the warm late afternoon Negev breeze. The atmosphere is so permeated with infectious joy that the very sun beams with happiness. My head feels light. As the procession winds through the dusty streets, people wave and clap. I have a déjà vu of a dream from many years ago where I entered the gates of a heavenly world, part of a procession to nirvana, that is how this procession feels.

We arrive at a decorated tent where a live band is playing. This would be my first Jewish wedding, although the customary traditions would not be observed as the location would need to be kosher, and Midburn decidedly is not.

A dancing crowd forms as the bride and groom are lifted up on shoulders to the cheers of all. Their faces speak pure rapture, two people who love each other deeply celebrating their love under the gaze of those dear to them. Friends, family, as well as new acquaintances and curious onlookers are all gathered; a Burner wedding is open to all.

The parents of the bride and groom are both present as well, stepping outside their comfort zone and into this strange environment to be there for their children. Their faces are also adorned with jewels and they look somewhat bewildered but endearingly happy, eager to bless the union.

The party dies down and the guests take their seats, cross-legged in the dusty comfort of the tent as we move to the official ceremony. Everyone is hushed as the groom and his parents walk down the aisle first and take their places waiting for the bride. The band plays a rendition of The Circle of Life, and radiant light from the setting sun filters gorgeously through the space. The groom and parents exchange a warm hug and nervous glances.

Suddenly the bride comes into view, and the groom goes to her so that both walk up the aisle together. They exchange vows in Hebrew, and in this moment crouched low in a dusty tent in a foreign land listening to a language I do not understand, a deep emotion takes hold. I do not grasp the meaning of the words, but instead deeply feel every inflection in the voice rising and falling as the declaration of love is shared. It dances with joy while retelling a happy moment, and movingly breaks with heartfelt emotion when recounting shared moments of intimacy.

The faces of the lovers and those in the room say a thousand words, eyes softening and laughing, at times stinging and misting over sweetly with tears. I do not need to strain to hear or understand what is said, I am simply experiencing the moment, two people speaking a universal language to each other. I am at once humbled and overwhelmed by the beauty of it, my body rocked by waves of chills.

This is my interpretation of the vows, what I heard them say beyond the words that day:

> *As I look into your eyes, I am like a child full of wonder, I am young and strong, I am old and wise. I am generations standing in front of you, carrying the same flame in my heart as those who came before me, asking for yours in return. The eyes of our parents beside us fill with tears and haze over like a water painting. Each brush stroke is a memory of love, a canvas full of whispered moments of intimacy, stretching back for millennia to the dawn of time.*
>
> *As I stand in front of you, I am also the mirror of those who will come after me. Our children and our children's children. I see*

their eyes in yours already, their smile in your smile. They will fall and we will pick them up to show them the way, but when they fall in love we will gently let go of their hand. We will let them go forth on the journey that exists only between two people, one that they will experience like second nature, instinctively felt through a generational web of emotions. Once fallen it is a journey they may never get up from again...

So it is not just me my love who stands in front of you today surrounded by the circle of love and life formed by our friends and family. I am every man and woman telling you a timeless story, one that binds the whole of humanity together. I am the water painting, I am the mirror, and yes, I am the fallen man.

I wrote this passage with my heart still full, still feeling the energy of the newlyweds like a warm embrace. It is a moment that would stay with me.

Nowadays weddings have become all too contrived, elaborate expensive affairs, a rite of passage to be observed for convention's sake. But here, in the simplicity of the surroundings and stripped bare of set traditions, I feel the cup overflowing with joy from a timeless and pure love.

Months later I would learn the symbolism of Jewish weddings and was struck at how this resonated with the words I wrote down on the day. On a cosmic level, the Jewish marriage ceremony is thought to reflect the relationship between all Jews and their God. The souls of the bride and groom reunite to become one soul as they were before entering the world. Every Jew is seen as part of the larger Jewish body, including all souls across generations, coming together through the union of the lovers. And so it was that day.

I wake up with a post-wedding hangover the next day. Memories of wild dancing, obscenely-shaped bread baked to raucous laughter, chili body shots, and bar hopping merge into one. Today is Thursday, which in Midburn is

Burn night. Friday is the temple Burn and the city is disbanded on Saturday for the Shabbat.

By now, the kitchen is churning out some sensational meals, the oven fired up and working hard. That afternoon we feast on fairly epic burgers prepared by the now-married groom, an outright delicacy in the middle of an arid desert. With an equally epic hangover, I turn up for trash aka MOOP duty for one of my camp shifts. We make a number of trips out to the edge of the Midburn playa carrying heavy bags in the absolutely searing heat. Despite my pounding headache, these moments of camp camaraderie are essential to the Burn experience. Co-creating a city cannot happen without communal effort.

Despite the heavy lifting and downright dirty job, we laugh and joke throughout. It helps that I have been paired with my hilarious randy camp-mate for the task. He darts around hauling heavy bags like a jack-in-the-box. After several trips, sweat is streaming down both of our bodies.

Suddenly, I spot a small trailer on wheels in a neighboring camp. "Can we borrow it?" I ask, "*Yallah*! Sure!" responds our long-haired neighbor. And without a moment's hesitation he joins in the task to help us carry the rest of the pungent bags to their final destination. How different the outside world would be if we all collaborated with each other as naturally as we do here.

MOOP duty done, I clean up and head back to camp. Though my hangover has not let up, and my head is heavy, my heart feels light from the wedding events of the previous day. It's as if it had dusted off and let down its guard while softly opening, imbued with a sense of calm and empathy. It is uncanny how an open heart lets in a flurry of deep connections.

Back in the shade of the circus tent where all manner of eccentrics are whiling away the hours in the heat of the day, I spot someone sitting alone in a corner quietly observing the scene: a middle-aged man, clean shaven and in normal attire, looking completely out of place. The living embodiment of the word *sachi* in Hebrew—conventional or mainstream. For some reason I am drawn to him and cross the tent to his side.

"Can I sit down?" I ask. As we talk, he begins to share his life outside of this dusty realm, timidly at first but then with growing confidence. "I have come here to get away from life, from stress," he says in heavily accented English. As a father of two with a failing business, he feels the weight of the world on his shoulders. A blend of social norms and toxic masculinity means he keeps his fears and anxieties tightly guarded and locked inside. His voice is choked as he reveals, "You are the second person I have spoken to since here, I guess people don't understand me."

I reach out and hold his hand. Surprised by this unexpected contact, his eyes mist over with tears. We sit in silence for a while in the shared emotional space. "I have not cried in ten years," he eventually admits almost inaudibly, eyes fixed on the floor. I press the hand in mine a little harder, hoping to signal that it is ok, that we have all felt fear and doubt, that every emotion is a lesson, and that this is a safe place.

So often the world tells us we must be strong, that we must rise above, clawing our way up if we need to and that any sign of weakness will be our downfall. Tired from the fight, we spend our lives bruised on the inside. Sometimes every beat hurts with the strain of existence. After a while, we speak again until the man stands up and we say our goodbyes. We do not exchange contact details, nor do I know his name, but this moment of shared anonymous intimacy gave us both some form of healing.

In many ways this is the real gift the Burn provides, across all continents. As we become united in dust, the desert has an infallible way of providing opportunities to open our souls and share intimate stories of human experiences which we usually keep bottled up in our everyday lives. A place to be vulnerable, to be understood. Our sprawling cities have given us models of society that sorely lack such spaces. The Burn environment is a pressure cooker for moments of transcendence, when, blindsided by artistic beauty and the energy of those that have created it, we go beyond the boundaries of the self to connect with others and a higher order. It is said that transcendent states lead to higher levels of oxytocin in the blood, the hormone that promotes bonding between two people.

Later this evening I will have another memorable experience, meeting a virgin Burner who explained how he survived a near-death experience which put him in coma for 19 days at this time last year. It was not yet his time, and he came back to life on his birthday, surrounded by family. Since then, he has faced an upward battle to make sense of this experience and rebuild cognitive abilities to reconstruct a life turned on its head.

He looks like an Israeli version of Che Guevara, with flowing dark hair and beard, and all the promise and hope of youth. You would never know by looking at him the grueling rehab he's been through. We talk for hours about second chances in life. Over a decade ago, I was dealt a tough blow, narrowly surviving an illness that would knock me sideways, jolting buried fears of life and death to the surface. As we shared stories, I realized just how much I had repressed the fallout from this event, and how it was still affecting my sense of self.

Even when meeting strangers, as innately social beings and in the right environment, we tend to respond to disclosure with disclosure. We are all fighting internal demons that we have learned to expertly mask with a smile during our day-to-day interactions. But from a position of shared vulnerability we let the mask slip long enough to create lasting bonds.

Beyond these two isolated stories, the Israeli people are dealing with a host of emotions from the strains of life in a contested land, a compulsory military service, or in some cases, having escaped the rigidity of a strictly religious family. In this charged environment a place for escape and healing is all the more critical.

All around me, crowds are gathering for the Burns which will mark the end of the week. The Burns here are spectacular, expertly timed and engineered with cutting-edge Israeli knowhow. The effigy of the tin soldier and ballerina explode together in a symphony of flames to the cheers of the crowd. In its final act, it celebrates fragility and togetherness. The soldier struck down in his prime is bound forever in immortal love to the ballerina.

The burning of such a powerful piece invariably moves its audience deeply. Later, a Midburn friend would reveal how he cried whilst it went up in flames, symbolically letting go of his best friend who had been diagnosed with terminal cancer, forced to face his own fragility. Like the tin soldier his friend stood still, rendered speechless by his treatment and trapped in limbo, motionlessly observing as the ballerina, his wife of six months, continued to dance. In his weakness she is his strength, dancing on to celebrate his life, dancing on when he is unable to. He stands stoically awaiting his fate, holding her in his sight as the music fades, knowing that this love will never die. In the tale, the soldier eventually melts into a tin heart. Whilst the strength of a body may be reduced to ashes, a heart that has loved lives on forever in those it has touched.

We gather for the Burn of the towering camel next. With outstretched straw wings and raised front hooves, it majestically hovers off the earth in mid-flight. As the fire is lit and dances around its swollen underbelly, the bark crackles and hisses like a panic-stricken animal. With growing fervor the trapped flames rattle deeply within the camel's rib cage, emblazing its desert-weary heart. As it audibly exhales its last dying breath a stream of bright sparks erupts loudly, pouring like lava from either side of its snout.

Suddenly possessed, the camel morphs into a giant fire breathing dragon, transformed from trustworthy king of the desert to fiery lord of the underworld. Its wings burst alight and behind the bushy feathered straw, thick clouds of billowing smoke elevate it higher into the night sky. Dragons have deep symbolism across cultures. In Hebrew folklore, the Babylonian story of Marduk's victory over the dragon of the sea, Tiamat, is used to symbolize the destruction of one's enemies. Perhaps the dragon represents all of our demons, which must be slain to finally set us free.

As the celebrations ramp up a notch, the whole of Midburn starts to resemble some wildly festive Purim party. Our campmates push an art car decked out with a powerful sound system and palm trees, serving onboard cocktails. Mayhem erupts and revelers dance to installations that beam brightly such as *Rabbits in the Sand*, a towering projection of three rabbits with tripped-out heads stacked on top of each other. There are gasps as a giant music organ, ingeniously crafted and played by its young maker, lights up the night sky with each brilliant note.

All around everyone is connecting with their inner child, the desert is alive with interactive creations, and laughter and glee abound as people set aside the strains of their daily lives and are finally allowed to play. Beyond the state-of-the-art creations, nothing says play like the Shoobi Doobi Camp—or Teddy Bear Camp, in Hebrew. Here, grown adults climb and rest on top of giant teddy bears. And then there's the Un-Birthday Camp, celebrating the other 364 days of the year.

Somewhat frayed at the edges but elated, I make it to sunrise, as the giant ball rises from the sand and floods the barren Negev desert with molten gold, sending the temperature soaring. I bump into a fellow desert wanderer before heading back to camp, and we end up whiling the hours away on large plush red cushions under a huge vagina-shaped dome at the aptly named Pussynema.

The Midburn event draws to a close that night. All around, Shabbat dinners are being celebrated, with friends and strangers gathered at large wooden tables.

As the temple burns, the giant wooden compass symbolizing the finding of one's path, I reflect on its significance and the lessons which the desert has imparted this week. I think of my own epic journey of self-discovery through three consecutive Burns. I have learned so much. Witnessing the people of Midburn, fiercely loyal and united, organized and seamlessly working together as one body with multiple arms, has taught me that by banding together we can lift ourselves to a position of strength.

I've also learned that one open heart attracts another, and that second chances in life are possible, but we must remember not to lose ourselves whilst reinventing our paths.

The exponential growth of the Midburn event is not accidental. It is deeply linked to the communal spirit which exists here, and the need for an outlet in a charged country. While the Burn's message of inclusion is still somewhat at odds with the prevailing reality, perhaps this is a sign of much-needed change.

The soft night air brushes our faces hot and dry, and the wilderness of Israel's desert expands outward in endless undulating dunes, reverberating with the sounds of ancient tongues. For days we have weathered its unforgiving sun and scorching sand, exploring the deep crevasses of this land steeped in history.

Judaism sees the divine as transcending nature, existing not in things seen, but in words heard, its culture a culture of the ear—of words, speech, listening, interpreting, understanding, heeding. The Torah suggests that God orchestrated the Jews' going into the desert because the atmosphere created in such desolate and lonely surroundings would be conducive to spiritual growth and reflection. It is said that in the desert, they became the People of the Word.

From time immemorial the desert has been a mystical place attracting visionaries and those rejecting urban society to commune with a higher order and develop their spiritual capacities. Out here where the world is stripped bare, exposed to the harshness of the elements, we test the boundaries of our humanity, connecting with the whole spectrum of our emotions.

Like the desert's constantly changing forms, its shifting sands travel great distances in sandy tidal waves, so our thoughts shape our world, ebbing and flowing to take us to different places in our minds. An endless time machine jumping from past to present and projecting us into images of a fabricated future.

We are all inexorably moving through emotions on the journey of life, with a constant push and pull between a need for exploration and renewal and a deep yearning for roots and belonging. It is the very journey through these emotions that shows us the path we must take. The barren desert canvas allows us to journey freely, and as we commune with others on their journeys, we glimpse new paths of possibility for our own. In this way we can find a third path, and make positive waves in our societies.

The last day is reserved for camp strike. Cirque du Shlapy is one of the larger camps and the many hoops and props used by the acrobats for their gravity defying tricks have to be taken down and stored. Midburn is a hive of activity as camps pack up, with most campmates in situ for the entirety of strike.

The temperatures have been building as the week has progressed, climbing to over 100°F at the height of the day. We start working at the crack of dawn. The campmate responsible for orchestrating the camp acrobats now leads the strike charge. With his usual humor he grabs his loudspeaker and hollers out a strident call at 6am to wake the sleeping camp. Tent doors are unzipped, and campmates emerge rubbing their eyes. Everyone stands to attention as dismantling tasks are assigned. The plan in place, we then busily get down to work like a well-regimented ant colony to pack away our home.

By midafternoon the heavy circus tent comes down leaving us with no shade. We start raking the Midburn sand, squinting in the sunlight while clearing any remaining trace or debris with military precision. An endless supply of ice-cold drinks is mercifully being handed out. My throat is like sandpaper and my temples pulse as I down can after can, the cool liquid streaming through my overheated body like nectar. As the punishing sun finally dips our work is almost done. One by one we start saying our good-byes. Sweaty hugs are exchanged, and I feel a lump rise in my throat. I know I will sorely miss this family of hardworking eccentrics with their huge smiles and brazen humor.

As we drive away, I scan the dismantling city and am astounded at the speed at which the whole site has almost completely been taken down. It is clear that in this culture no one stands idly on the sidelines during the hard work. As with all Burn events, the work does not stop when the camps have packed up. An army of volunteers stays onsite to ensure there is absolutely no trace left across the event site. The city needs to vanish completely for it to be born anew the following year.

Of all the Burns I would attend, perhaps Midburn would leave the deepest mark. After participating in three consecutive Burns and social experiments, I could feel my mindset shift. I felt a renewed sense of positivity and possibility that the outside world had dulled. I decided then and there that I would no longer work an office job. A few weeks later I serendipitously landed a contract working remotely, long before the pandemic made this commonplace.

Most importantly, the connections I made in the Negev slowly started taking my guard down. The moments of anonymous disclosure I shared with the two strangers after the wedding, and my friend's experience of the effigy Burn played over in my mind. The courage they had shown in their vulnerability, opening up about their deeply personal stories would stay with me. As Larry Harvey once said, "What makes a life worth living is a meaningful connection to the world and other people, what else?"

As my journey progressed, I would increasingly be moved by the temples I would encounter, and the way they provided healing spaces regardless of the culture they were built in. Here, the Compass's call to self-discovery and finding your way seemed to perfectly encapsulate the journey of its desert-hardy people. And this in turn made me reflect on my own.

Chapter 4:
Nowhere

SPAIN — 2-8 JULY 2018

*A*fter clocking three Regionals in three months, I have a 6-week break until the European edition of my Regional tour. I feel both elated and spent at this mid-way point. Instead of taking time for a much-needed rest, I head to two city festivals in Barcelona. Still in a Burn mindset, I try to playfully engage people, forgetting that different rules apply in the default world. Sadly, I am reminded that people tend to be far more insular in their friendship groups outside of the Burn context.

There is a tight-knit Burning Man community in Barcelona, and I go to several of their events and regular meetups, including a house party in a stunning *casa rural* or country house outside of the city which ends in fun, games and glow in the dark paint on every single body and wall.

A tribute party in honor of Larry Harvey, who had passed away a few months earlier, is held on a full moon night in June before the main event. As the city faces east, the moon rises glowing pink over the ocean as a backdrop to the encroaching twilight. After the long hot day, we bask in the balmy summer night, and write intentions and stories on colored paper handed to us by the organizers. These are shared aloud or kept secret and gifted to others folded into small envelopes.

As July arrives, I prepare for the Nowhere event, which takes place in the arid Monegros Desert in Northeastern Spain. Because of its size as one of the largest Burn gatherings in Europe it attracts people from all over the continent seeking a local Burning Man experience. In a time where Europe seems to be imploding, it is as if a mini European Union has sprung up quite literally in the middle of Nowhere. Although located in Spain, the chatter of dozens of European voices rises over the makeshift camps or *barrios,* with French being a dominant strain the year I attended.

The first edition of Nowhere was in 2004. It was originally organized by UK-based Burners as a Decompression event, and has taken place annually in July since. Despite being held for over a decade its population peaked at around 3,600 people. Due to the dry area of the Monegros desert, which is on wildfire alert during the summer, any kind of open fire is forbidden, therefore no art is set alight during the event.

During the summer months the air fills with large swarms of ravenous mosquitoes at dusk. The desert here, really more of a plain, is not nearly as inhospitable to life as is the one in Nevada. In fact, once upon a time the Monegros was not a desert at all; the area was deforested centuries ago to supply timber to build ships for the Spanish Armada. A whole forest evaporated into ships. Ever since, the land has been left barren and prone to flash flooding; this also makes it a feasting ground for mosquitoes and insects.

Although it abides by the Burning Man principles, Nowhere seems to be rooted in the European free-party or rave scene. Nowhere is the European counterculture seeking to shake the establishment. It is extreme because civilization here has come full circle and is now violently questioning its broken social norms, with people rejecting the status quo. Nowadays, the European continent is in decline, opinions of its populations are polarizing and groups are becoming more insular. This is threatening to break its very union apart, leaving the current generation in a crisis of identity.

After going to three consecutive Burning Man Regionals and playing a balancing act with work, I am unfortunately not able to take a week off to attend the full Nowhere event, and so arrive early on Friday. This means I have missed the buildup and gradual immersion which unfolded earlier in the week.

Perhaps this explains why I was blown away by the intensity of what I found at Nowhere on arrival. When there has been no warmup, it is hard to hit the ground running without a sprain. I am told that there is a virgin ritual to complete if it is your first time at Nowhere which is to hit the *Gong Butanero,* a gong made out of a propane canister. Sadly, I arrive too late in the week to officially lose my Nowhere virginity before the event starts.

Here, I am free-camping rather than staying with one of the established camps but, given my other Regional experiences, am confident I will be welcomed into the Nowhere family. As the summer is in full swing, I travel light leaving my warm gear at home. I drive in with another Nowhere virgin and a tiny tent that I would not even put up, too busy processing the extreme environment I would soon experience.

My arrival at Nowhere is like being instantly immersed in a wild Mad Max fantasy sequence; the first scene I witness is a woman, completely naked, being paraded around by five men before being tied to a stake in broad daylight. In medieval fashion, they pelt her naked body and face with mud as she writhes on the pole.

As I turn away another scene is unfolding in a nearby camp, the Nowhere equivalent of the Thunderdome found in Black Rock City. This is similar in that the fighters are strapped in harnesses for aerial battle, but has a much more raw sexual energy as they are barely clothed, and the fighting is done with bare hands.

This sets the tone for what's to come. At this European Burn, radical self-expression has translated into organized anarchy where a desire to let loose is omnipresent. I have arrived at the weekend when the celebrations are in full swing.

In the heat of the day, only the most intrepid leave their hiding places to explore the scorched grounds, flanked by hot plumes of dust rising like mini-tornados. As the temperatures cool, a sea of people emerge to mill around the playa giggling and clambering perilously to the top of giant containers to stare at the emptiness of space. As night falls, the sun sets behind the Monegros hills, and a giant fan-like cloud is painted shades of sunset pink and hangs suspended in the air as if magically propped on the mountain top. I pass a large sign that reads out "Will you Marry Me?" At the time I did not know this was a proposal from two of the campmates from the Here and Now Camp. I would later find out that the campmates married and were later to have two children together. A Nowhere happy ending.

As day turns to night and the shenanigans amplify, I lose sight of my car companion and all hope of putting up my tent. I meet a friend from my hometown staying in one of the established *barrios* with his campmates, and we venture out in the direction of the sound camps.

The Nowhere playground has a distinct steampunk feel at night. It feels like anything goes, with a raw energy unlike the other Burns I have attended this year. As I step into the fray, my gaze turns upwards to two huge circular metal cages welded together like an apocalyptic fairground attraction. It is powered by a pulley system, activated when participants enter the cages and start walking. As the wheels spin, fire is propelled into the air in controlled explosions by four fire cannons attached to its center. An indelible image is imprinted in my mind as a participant in the top cage spreads his arm victoriously and howls, illuminated by fire spewing from the cannons. The whole crowd howls back. Fuck yeah.

I imagine that this is what Burning Man would have been like 20 years ago. It is exhilarating.

Later that night the installation serves as a backdrop to a fire spinning show. A brazen woman appears dancing rhythmically with two fire fans, hypnotizing us all with her expertly sequenced movements. Next up is a beast of a man with long dark hair and muscular arms, looking straight out of a Vikings sequence. As he starts spinning, the chorus of "Let it Go" from the Disney film *Frozen* suddenly blasts out of the speakers comically to the hilarity of all. As I scan the crowd, I notice that not a single person has taken their phone out to film the sequence. Everyone is too absorbed in living in the present moment. How rare and refreshing this is.

Wandering the grounds after the performance I stumble upon a cart manned by an eclectic character in an Alice in Wonderland dress. He opens a secret compartment in the cart revealing a whole assortment of whiskies. I avoid getting trapped in the rabbit hole, and instead retreat to my friend's tent which has been decked out with a real mattress and cozy decorations. It would be the only decent night of sleep I would have at Nowhere.

The next day I have breakfast at my friend's *barrio*, Camp Now, and connect with a slower pace and community energy. Nowhere has a more laid-back feel during the day, and today the playa is particularly quiet as its citizens are nursing major hangovers. The *barrios* are tightly knit, and the residents work collaboratively. Officially, the inhabitants of Nowhere are called "Nobodies," but they affectionately and self-deprecatingly refer to each other as "hippies." There is a big neo-hippie culture in Spain, notably in nearby Barcelona or the island of Ibiza, and outside the event attendees meet regularly at spiritual wellness type workshops such as ecstatic dance, sound healing, or tantra.

That said, the *barrio* culture seems to be somewhat more insular than what I've experienced at other Burns. Here people are not as quick to welcome strangers in and offerings such as food are not as willingly gifted. This could be a natural backlash to the scale of the non-aligned or "free-camping" population at Nowhere, which is a higher percentage than at other Burns. Or it may be down to the awkwardness that some of us Europeans feel when faced with strangers.

I make a new friend and we find shade under the cover of an art structure before heading to the costume camp. Amongst the rails of colorful costumes that one is free to borrow and return, I happily spot an old friend from Fuego Austral by his trademark huge blonde afro, and we share a heartfelt hug in the midday sun before we each go on our way.

Within the first hour of meeting, the conversation with my new friend has already turned suggestive. "Are you into bondage and S&M?" I am asked. When I politely decline the invitation I am told to "give it a try." His persistence makes me uncomfortable. This exchange highlights the importance of consent in such a liberated sex-positive environment.

Consent is something the community needs to have an open and continuous dialog on. And fortunately, it seems that around the Regional Network it has, with leadership actively facilitating discussion, solutions, and best practices for creating environments where consent and boundaries are safe and respected.

Some Regionals have even added consent—in all its forms—as an 11th principle. Burning Man is intrinsically responsive to the cultural issues in our wider society that matter to participants. The addition of this principle shows that the community continues to move organically in line with the times. While a liberated environment can be extraordinarily positive, a balance needs to be struck between one's radical self-expression and everyone else's.

The rest of the afternoon is spent cruising around and finding our bearings, either by foot or hitching a ride on the few stray art cars. There are some colorful costumes here, but given the stifling heat, most bodies are bare. Some are painted in body art like beautiful fleshy canvases. Myriad colored butterfly wings stretched and rounded over curves, taking off in flight.

Participants seem particularly adept at the art of self-derision and pranks. I witness a lively and humorous exchange between a curly-haired blond girl trying to purchase a piece of camp land from a bewildered looking hippie using "klepto-currency." "Name your price!" she bellows as she starts writing out her klepto cheque. Inspired.

Unlike BRC, Nowhere does not have a Burn as its main culminating community ritual due to fire restrictions in the Monegros desert. It uses a lighthouse as its effigy and a compass as its logo, and the center camp is appropriately named Middle of Nowhere. The event uses a layout that reassembles a compass. This leads to an arrangement of the *barrios* in a circular shape, unlike Burning Man's semi-circular layout in Nevada.

I am told the lighthouse was burnt in the 2016 edition when the organizers came to an agreement with the local authorities. However, no Burns take place in the 2018 Nowhere edition. The non-burning policy means that all the art needs to be dismantled, removed, and stored after the event, which translates into fewer large artworks on display than in BRC. The art that one does see dotted around the earthy playa often has a sarcastic twist, adding humor to the whimsical world around us. I pass a robot head that hangs attached to two wires, and sit on the stool positioned underneath. Putting my head in it is like entering a psychedelia of lights where reality and the desert fall away for an LED-filled moment.

There are many sex-positive workshops offered, with diverse topics such as live lessons in cunnilingus, amongst others. But, there are also meditation, yoga, and sustainability workshops, which speak to the softer side of Nowhere. Others are just wonderful and silly.

Some of the art installations, though simple, are touching, and resonate with the search for connection that is so pervasive across the Burns. *The Lovebox* is an art installation with two doors. Dusty strangers enter on either side to look into each other's eyes, and tell the other what they see. The box acts like a confessional and in this vulnerable and private space something is cracked open. Secrets are shared and connections are made with the strangers who see us, but know nothing about us. At the end hugs are exchanged.

I have some beautiful exchanges about togetherness with people here. I have since been inspired by the Barcelona Burner community and the way the Nowhere residents and Barcelona crews rally together, get creative and take Burner culture back to their city.

This tight group of creative and free thinkers represent a generation that is striving to find solutions, putting their brain power into trying to solve some of the problems of our time, be they environmental or social. I speak to a participant creating a value-based framework to apply to corporate settings which can be scaled up to governments. I chat with another about a project tackling plastic pollution on Spain's beaches.

Let us not forget that the organizers of Nowhere spend hundreds of hours planning and building, and do so entirely for free. There is no undercover police force patrolling as can be found in the American and Israeli versions. But because it is not sanitized or completely safe, attendees are allowed unbridled freedom and get to practice complete self-reliance. There are reports that a string of hammocks once collapsed at Ubertown, one of the largest *barrios*, resulting in an injury. The organizers footed the medical bill as a gift.

One thing that feels constant across all Burns is a worship of the sunset. At dusk, we leave the camp area to climb one of the surrounding hills, following a procession of hippies. The air is still and cool and the many faces at the summit smile.

As there is no Burn on any night at Nowhere, the setting sun is the main event, the ritual that we howl to. It is the most beautiful and timeless sort of Burn, giving sense to our very existence. I reflect on what life would be without the sun, if it were to stop rising suddenly one day, and we woke to darkness. Then, there would be no life at all. Every day that we welcome in and wave off the sun, we are blessed, and when we take the time to celebrate its cycles among our human tribe its energy passes through us all like seven billion blessings.

That night an almighty desert storm rains down heavily on this previously forested land. As the whole site becomes a mud bath, Nobodies drop to the ground to roll in it. We slide precariously, moving between sound camps. In the darkness I almost trip over a couple writhing around in it.

We seek sanctuary from the storm in a colorful bus stationed in the middle of the playa. "Where are you going?" asks the leather-clad driver in a heavily accented German voice. "Umm, Nowhere?" we reply with a smile. "Wunderbar! Hop on!" And with that we board the stationary bus marooned in mud to join an animated party. It feels decidedly more like being in Munich than a desert in Spain.

Later that night we find ourselves in a tent in full bacchanalia. The Garden of Joy is one of the main *barrios* and has a dance floor in its center, but if one tries to make sense of the shadows, multiple love-making scenes are taking place on the cushions surrounding it. A tangle of limbs plays out in the backdrop, as electronic music pounds relentlessly, the bass hitting every nerve end.

Tired and spent from the day's events, I walk away from the madness and am drawn to a quiet neighboring camp. It is empty aside from a *Nobody* playing the piano. The soothing and melancholy notes ring out, a contrast to the hyper-stimulating environment I was in moments before. I stop to listen. As I am about to gather my things to leave a strange man suddenly appears across the empty camp dancefloor. He is wearing a black cape, dark mittens, and an eerie looking mask and headpiece. Even his eyes are hidden behind circular LED lights. It is like he has landed from another planet. A Star Wars-esque version of the grim reaper.

We instinctively move towards each other slowly, in sync with the dramatic notes of the piano. Without a word we come together. We join hands and start to dance within the empty space. I stare into the LED rimmed eyes of this mysterious being as we move, wondering what face hides behind the mask. Finally he says to me in a low and gentle voice "it is not your time yet." I feel a chill of wonder down my spine. He squeezes my hands lightly before bringing his palms together and bowing his head solemnly to bid me farewell. He then disappears into the cool night.

Our lives are so one dimensional, firmly fixed in reality with far too little intrigue and play. I do not know what this strange encounter meant, I just know that it moved me. For a moment, I stripped away my default conditioning to dance with a cloaked messenger from another galaxy. And time stood still. As I walk away still dazed by the encounter, the soft notes of the piano music grow fainter in the night.

The next day it is already time to leave. Given I am free-camping, and have not even had time to put up a tent in these frenzied days, I have no strike duties. We drive back home with a dominatrix and slave who have hitched a ride with us. A fitting Nowhere-leaving party.

Although it only lasts three days, my time at Nowhere is intense. Having not experienced the build-up of the event earlier in the week or joined an established camp, my experience of the community spirit here feels more muted than other Burns. This is a reminder that more time is required to create bonds and have a meaningful Burn experience. The so-called "weekend warriors" who do not contribute to event setup and co-creation only leave with a limited amount of the magic it can provide.

But even in a short space of time I felt the rawness and authenticity of this playa. It is a city that pulses with energy, a melting pot for the many European cultures that flock to it. It blends the culture of Cacophony and play at the core of Burning Man's early philosophy with that of new age spirituality; the latter now a stalwart of the movement in its own right. Its camps are full of hot bodies, cold beverages, heckling and hilarity. But its workshops and smaller scale art are full of meaning and intention.

A softer side dominates Nowhere by day, but at night it is filled with mind-bending mayhem. There is no burning of structures as a ritual, usually so central to the Burn experience, yet fire seems to literally fuel its participants. There is a no-holds-barred approach to revelry in all its forms. While the event is unashamedly sex-positive, consent is taken seriously across the network, including at Nowhere. The event offers a space to leave inhibitions aside and explore aspects of ourselves that are repressed in our day-to-day lives. This micro-community brings sexual liberation and acceptance of all forms of sexual expression into the norm. This aspect of dialogue and normalization helps to break down taboos.

Unlike the other Burns I would attend that year, Nowhere has no temple. Its absence is puzzling, especially given modern European culture generally lacks clear frameworks for grieving—which are therefore all the more needed. There is no time for reflection when one is busy living so intensely.

Still, away from the maddening crowds, strange beings from other galaxies come to deliver cryptic messages that feel like sacred experiences in themselves. Perhaps we don't need temples or rituals, but simply connections with each other in order to feel magic and transcendent experiences.

If we pick the name Nowhere apart we can also read "Now Here." This place, with its wild abandon, asks us to give in to the present moment and leave conventions at the door. This short and intense Burn experience taught me about myself: where my boundaries lie, my hang ups, and the importance of a healthy dialogue around consent and safe spaces in Burn venues. It also gave me moments of play that made me laugh till I cry, and surprising times of reflection and beauty beyond the madness.

Chapter 5:
Black Rock City

USA – 26 AUGUST - 3 SEPTEMBER 2018

Back on the Burn preparation train. I'll be camping with the Brazilian camp this year: AmaZONE. While I attended most of the Regional Burns solo, I have come to BRC with a group of my closest friends. A two-month hiatus has served me well and the excitement builds up again. I'm like a small child before Christmas, playing the possible events over in my head. What will the playa offer this year? That white dusty bowl sitting in stillness in an inhospitable desert, lying in wait. Soon the pilgrims will arrive, busily erecting wondrous playthings and creations conceived over months in all corners of the world. I am ready for the main course, the Burn that has led the way for all the Regionals to emulate.

This US Burn has a special tug as the origin point where all Burns began. We snake through the Californian landscape toward the Nevada desert as excitement mounts. The pull of home, that familiar tug towards an ethereal place that springs up yearly like Brigadoon: a magical place only accessible for a brief moment in time.

Around a bend the horizon suddenly opens, the mountains lining the road giving way to a vast expanse of desert wilderness, a beautiful bowl of powdery white dust, smoothed and stretched out like a lunar painting. As we approach the gate, the road winds from tarmac into desert, dust blowing across it silently, repossessing it slowly, the man-made giving way to nature.

Looking forward now, the still mind accelerates. This morning feels like a lifetime ago, like we are wholly new. We enter our communal land, ¨home¨ as some people affectionately refer to it, savoring the thought of seven full sunsets and sunrises here. We will shiver together as the night turns to day, huddled closely, breathlessly, awaiting the sun god who will fill the sky and shower the cracked earth with gold sparks. Gold sparks that penetrate it deeply, giving off pink hues. Hairs on arms rise with the anticipation of it all.

Finally here, all the waiting, all the planning done. 80,000 hopeful hearts ready to give their all to this week. Running into the unknown, running into the madness that awaits us. That delicious unstructured madness…all emotions will blend and be accentuated this week; we will laugh till we cry, weep with exhaustion, fall in love a million times, feel disappointed, over-stimulated, mad and lost. We will play intensely, and feel overwhelmed by nostalgia in trying to bottle it all up and take it away with us. We will live so immediately that we will feel others living next to us, eyes dancing, hearts swaying, blood racing, senses overloaded with beauty.

Black Rock City has its roots in the San Francisco hippie ethos of the 60s, and a desire for wild abandon. The need to escape a rigid system that was no longer working, that a whole generation no longer identified with. Drugs had their place in the hippie order, but were not the whole of it, just as it is with Burning Man. The drug notion is often a channel used by critics to judge and undermine both movements, but they have missed the point. Burning Man, or Black Rock City, is not solely a playground attracting recreational drug users, but has a deeper meaning altogether. Above all, people flock to this community to make human connections. This is the real intoxicant of the playa.

The BRC event has a particularly US flavor. Everything is big here: the art, the lights, the events, the flamboyance of the costumes, the theatrical mise en scene of camps and passers-by, and most of all, the oversized personalities.

Because of this, it is in some ways more intense than the Regionals, like grabbing a rodeo bull by the horns and holding on for dear life. The full immersion and mind-bending plethora of options means that every attendee can create their very own customized experience of the event. You can spend a whole week rising at 6am for sun salutations and meditation; enjoy a week-long wholesome dusty camping trip with the family, inviting your neighbors over for dinners; circle and experience an abundance of art revealed in a dust-veiled museum tour; stick to the backstreets and workshops and avoid the electronic rumblings of the Esplanade or deep playa altogether; or bid each day farewell well past sunrise with red-rimmed eyes and ringing in your ears after partying like a fiend all night. It is all possible in the same space; and as a side effect of living in a limitless world, somewhere along the way you start to change.

You are free to pick and mix, like a real life version of a "choose your own adventure" book where you can skip to the page you want and craft your own journey. Because of this, writing about the experience came forth in a stream of consciousness, trying to stay faithful to and convey that feeling of awesome acceleration of a week on another planet. If you get lost in the detail, you can move on to the next passage, just as you would dust yourself off and head to the next adventure of your choosing on the BRC Nevada playa.

If you are prone to bouts of FOMO like I am, you will spend the week depleting all of your energy stocks trying to do it all, fully living the highs and lows. I emerge from the week manically with a full heart, a bursting to the seams memory bank, cracked hands and feet, and impossibly dust-filled dreadlocked hair that I fear I have to chop off at the end of each stint at BRC. I'm not sure I ever fully decompress.

However you choose to experience this unique out-of-this-world space, make sure to turn off that phone, give and receive gifts, take time for solo missions, get dusty and speak to strangers! And whatever you do avoid paying exorbitant amounts for a 5-star "plug and play" experience, which the organization is rightly cracking down on. If you treat Burning Man like a resort, you will miss out on all its transformational power.

So grab my hand, hold on tight and strap in for my version of the ride.

Arriving on the playa is like stepping onto a rollercoaster, equal parts thrilling and exhausting, and from which one emerges at the end of the week completely spent. On the Burner Express bus we fly through the gate, bypassing the queue slowly pulsing in and are suddenly inside. Once in, the previous 48 hours start to take their toll.

I carry a week's worth of what I've accumulated: an excess of shiny fabrics, lights, furs, trinkets. A bag resembling a child's dress up chest, filled to the brim with eccentricity and playful fun. But right now it is heavy as hell and I sulk as I pull it through the dust, particularly sullen as I realize I've left my meal on the bus.

Barely a moment passes without a reminder that here I am not alone. Strangers invite me in for some warm food and warmer conversation. We sit together around a fire like family. A man named Warren with a serious face that unexpectedly cracks into a shrill childlike laugh each time his amusement is tickled defuses all of the stresses of the day. Our new friends then drive me back to my camp in a golf cart, which my imagination fashions as a dolphin crashing through the waves. After struggling to put up my tent for what seems like an eternity, I crash out to sleep.

I awaken, my face cracking into a smile at being "home." After a mouthful of dried nuts and fruits I clamber onto my bike and head out with a campmate, too excited to stay still. As the heat of the day rises, so too does the dust.

An almighty whiteout brews and swirls around the playa with force. Caught out in the thick of it, under our scarves and goggles we are all smiles. A playa whiteout has an eerie feel, like time standing still and all sense of direction erased. Cycling through it, every clean nook and cranny of our being is permeated with fine dust, a reminder from the playa that it is omnipresent, that it will creep into our bodies until it possesses our souls.

The dust rises and parts like a curtain, and through its clearings, sculptures magically appear before being veiled again in an ethereal dance. The crews erecting the Man and Temple are battered by the dust storm and construction is put on hold. The playa decides when it is ready to welcome its new visitors, and now it is running the show and calling the shots. Those lined up to enter the event today find themselves stuck in a never-ending backlog of cars, slowly crawling in for 11 hours.

The city is laid out in a broken circle around the Man. We follow the radial streets labeled with clock time to the Esplanade, the innermost street, which looks out to the desert. The other street names change each year, based on the year's art theme.

Despite the storm that rages around us, the city continues to rise, a beehive of activity. An artist paints a large, awe-inspiring mural in the thick of it, dust blending with the colors of her palette. Other Burners cycle through, exploring the playa, barely distinguishable under their desert attire, any sound from their spinning wheels muffled.

We spend hours wandering through the dusty day on various dusty adventures, stopping for a respite from it all and a cold drink at Center Camp and Media Mecca.

Although as experienced Burners we revel in this surreal world we have entered, newcomers are often bewildered and disoriented. A weary girl slumps in the corner of the information camp looking equal parts spent and despairing, but this is where the community magic comes in. Each helps the other find their playa feet. We sit and listen to her tale and soothe her with kind words and rainbow notes. As the day draws to a close we retreat to the warmth of our camp to meet and talk with our newfound family.

Monday wakes up dead still, all beauty and blue skies. The mountains tower over and frame the playa, pretty as a picture. Deep playa is an empty desert filled with a dizzying array of art installations. The art pieces that were veiled like a closed exhibition yesterday are now visible in all their splendor. A giant rainbow to climb over, a large polar bear, a crooked house, two lovers locked in an embrace…the list goes on. A playground ripe for the imagination to soar, a place where one can reconnect with the child inside, where one can marvel at the human spirit and creativity, all laid out in an other-worldly landscape.

Each wonderful human lucky enough to enjoy this space is decked out in an equally playful outfit, shimmery and iridescent fabrics glowing under the hot playa sun, beautiful flesh proudly on show. The scene is like the world spun on its head, the antithesis of the uniformed gray world we inhabit off playa. Here everything is bold, gorgeous, confident. A symphony of individuality and statements that scream, "I am here, this is me at my best."

Exploring side streets with my campmates again, it is scorchingly hot and we spot a shaded tunnel. It has been fashioned as a jungle, complete with mist and sounds of tropical birds happily chirping. Ingenious. Clutching the WhatWhereWhen playa guidebook like a bible, we scan its many offerings and circle the ones we intend to go to, in the knowledge that we would probably only go to about 10% of these. The playa is fickle and foils the best laid plans.

Still the week is young, and we make it to a tiara-making class where a man decked out in a princess gown teaches us the finer points of beading. We instantly experience a sense that we are back in preschool, and it feels glorious.

The rest of the day is spent exploring various crannies of the city, finding bars that have sprung up to serve free beverages for the week. We are beckoned to a Monday make-out session before riding to the Dude Happy Hour with mouths that feel like sandpaper from the relentless heat. A queue of around 50 Burners wearing characteristic *Big Lebowski* robes stands in a fairly orderly fashion waiting for the White Russians being served up. We all sit on rugs a la The Dude.

Having not completely switched over to Burn mode yet, at times I feel shy about joining in. The mind needs to adapt to the madness around, to ease into it all. And yet I'm already aware that despite the initial difficulty diving in, we will miss it all immensely once we have left.

As we cycle through our first playa sunset this becomes poignantly apparent, and we marvel at the scene. Everything is stained pink by the setting sun: the art, the faces, the horizon. The coolness of the air feels marvelous, and my head spins just that little bit faster.

Back at camp the weariness of a day cycling in crazy hot temperatures starts to take its toll, and just like that I start questioning the magic. As I lie in my tent, sounds coming in from three different stages, the mild onset of paranoia kicks in. I cannot help but think this is overwhelming, an assault to the senses, for good and bad. Sometimes we need that warm island safe and grounded in the eye of the storm as the world goes topsy-turvy around it.

Amidst strangers I start to crave a familiar face. The playa gives you sweet and tough love. It tests your limits and boundaries, pushes you to the edge of joy and despair all in the same day. Makes you love and hate yourself in the same hour. All emotions are heightened beyond belief, sometimes beyond what one can cope with. The Burn can be a manic-depressive episode constantly pushing you outside of your comfort zone. With its focus on immediacy it demands everything from you in the now, without respite. And this is why it such a good teacher of your limits.

In the dead of night I try and fail to find my friends at an LGBT and dungeon gathering. The playa works in mysterious ways, as those experiences may well have pushed me over the edge. But then I cycle back to the love I need in Center Camp, and take a time out over a hot drink.

Finally back with my campmates, we reconnect and talk of our experiences of the day, wrapped up in our furs, expelling all the negative thoughts. Just like in the rest of the world, sometimes we need to step off the daily grind rollercoaster and recoup; the body and soul demand it.

Often we do not listen and we end up spent and burnt out. Here at least the community will prop you up to remind you of this. Out there in our modern world, it seems there is barely time to connect with others as we spin in the wheel. The playa gives you downtime to listen and connect and hold each other up.

Away from technology and phones it is so much easier to have an uninterrupted conversation with another human, so simple yet so precious for well-being. And something that we are gradually losing touch with as we stare into the emptiness of our screens. We also interpret immediacy as wanting to do everything at once to be present in the moment, to consume all the experiences we can. Again, the playa teaches that this is unachievable by slowing one down with its harsh climate, forcing one to seek rest.

Even as I write this I realize I had the Burn that I needed and not the one I wanted. In the fast-paced world I try to do everything at once and burn both ends of the candle, feeling regret if I don't achieve things instantly. That is how I have interpreted the principle of Immediacy, but with hindsight I realize I have missed the point. Immediacy is as much about taking the time to stop and reflect as for taking action in the present moment.

I also realize the importance of spending time to appreciate loved ones rather than always seeking out new and thrilling experiences with strangers. Wisdom can just as well be found at home as out in the world; a nurturing environment is crucial for growth. I thank the playa for this lesson.

But, it is day two on the playa rollercoaster and I am still looking for excitement. I sleep badly and awake sleepily; the pace is relentless as I try to cram too many experiences into a week. Wearing my Tuesday tutu, as is a custom here, I hop on an art tour, boarding a giant sailing boat to take us around the playa.

Cruising around, the art comes to life. We learn the backstories of the artists and of their efforts to bring some of these monumental pieces to the desert. Among these is *The Desert God,* a 30-meter-tall Mongolian statue, giant puppets by a Spanish artist, a ginormous iridescent jellyfish that's still incomplete as it has been put up in a 'cursed' spot on the playa, a freakish representation of mother nature emerging from a robot with straw-like tentacled arms raised high in the air, stacked up cars swaying dangerously as people clamber onto them to the bar at its peak. This installation, straight out of Mad Max, would close later in the week as one of the cars bent in half!

One installation in particular strikes a chord: an afro-pick with a raised fist at the end titled *Power to All People*. It is beautifully crafted and not draped with a thousand LEDs like some of the pieces. It is powerful and understated, and speaks to the growing numbers of people of color attending the event despite the critical voices that—perhaps rightly—decry its lack of racial diversity. I hope it will lead the way for ever more diversity and radical inclusion.

A mad reveler suddenly interrupts this cultural affair by climbing onto the mast of a passing ship, hollering wildly at the participants before being heckled off. Only at the Burn.

Gearing up for sunset number two, my campmates and I head to a performance of the city's philharmonic orchestra. It is in fact an entire orchestra that has come to play for us, but its members are not wearing black suits as one might expect. No, the conductor is wearing a billowing green tutu with red boxers underneath. We are transported by the music filling the warm playa air, smiles all around. The sunset is a beautiful backdrop to the scene.

The concert has a further playa twist as the band throws hundreds of colorful kazoos into the air, in shades of electric pink and green, gold and deep blue, flying overhead and whistling like paper airplanes. Some scatter to the ground and are seized in the dust, others are caught mid-air by hundreds of hands. These wonderful beings are mostly observing the Tutu-Tuesday dress mode and as Beethoven's *Für Elise* rings out, a cacophony of tutu'd humans kazoo along to the music.

You could very rightly say that we were utterly butchering the song but at this precise moment it feels like our anthem, and all of us are equally and deliciously eccentric adult-sized children blowing into the kazoos at the top of our lungs. It is a glorious slapstick in the face of those stiff-upper-lip prigs who sit in silence and loudly *shushhh* when someone makes the most minute sound in a concert hall. Here we are merry and united in a ridiculous sing-along. Ah sweet, sweet playa magic.

With the kazoos still ringing in our ears and flapping inside the corners of our trinket-filled bags we go back to camp to change into our night attire, which mostly consists of fur and more colored fur, with some face jewels thrown in for good measure. As we head out into the night, we realize there is not one moon but two. High up in the sky, a giant glowing moon-sphere, half lit, half black, unevenly surfaced, can be seen. It is suspended in such a way that it sometimes becomes a crescent, an eclipse, or a full moon. We have made plans to meet at our camp's art piece, *The Altar of Intentions*, but in characteristic Burn fashion, no one is at the meeting spot when we show up.

And then, playa serendipity happens in all its glory and blindsides us. From afar we see a swarm of a hundred lights rising up slowly from the deepest playa's dusty vastness. Drawn by this magnetic force we make a bee-line for it, hearts pounding softly and steadily, eyes opening wide to drink in and savor the vision.

Thousands of luminous dots suddenly levitate into the ink-black night like a flurry of fireflies. Almost on cue, beautiful classical piano music fills the air and the fireflies dance and sway in perfect harmony, mirroring each soul-wrenching note and electrifying our senses. The drones move in unison, in delicate formation, turning various shades of white, pink, and deepest purple.

We stand hypnotized, possessed by the powerful visual scene, absorbed by the music. My heart rises like a lump in my throat, tears sweetly stinging my eyes. As if by magic, the wondrous apparition drops and disappears, reabsorbed into the darkness.

As the cheers rise and fall from the crowd, the mood shifts as the Mayan Warrior, one of the largest sound art cars on the playa, takes over. Chills fill every inch of my being against the warm night air. Deep tribal beats rise from the Warrior's belly, barely letting me recover. With my campmates, we cycle with it, our master for the night, pounding us with bass that makes the ground rumble and its followers purr. And just like that I am hopelessly lost to the acceleration of the week, the default world firmly behind me, heart wide open to receive every glorious moment of playa magic, to feel and abandon myself to every connection. To being "home" again.

With love in our hearts we cycle to the Man, as is fitting to do. The first glimpse of it from the bottom of the stairs is awe-inspiring. The Man sits atop a temple, like an Aztec sacrificial scene. The stairs are steep, almost vertical; we ascend them slowly and notice the deep engravings on either side, as if robots have carved their indecipherable writings on each step, backlit by LEDs. I feel small walking up the stairs.

The Man is chained to this temple from all four sides, a prisoner of the robots, upright on the altar, about to be sacrificed. Each attendee has their own special bond to the Man, which acts as the epicenter of our experience. It was the original art piece, and the symbol of the movement.

The experience that each one of us has and the interpretation of its significance is lived differently. As I gaze up those stairs at the Man in chains, I see this year's "I, Robot" theme as a warning, a negative force. The machines have a hold on us, deeper than we imagined when we dreamt them up. The writing is on the wall, but we are unable to read the warnings scrolled across the altar in alien language.

Poignantly, the Man stands alone and vulnerable surrounded by these powerful forces. And within the structure to which it is chained video messages are screened, encircling it. It stands outside, exposed, while the robots shelter below, hatching their sacrificial plan. There would need to be a collective effort to save it, but all are too busy, absorbed by the technology and bright images to take notice.

More than ever, this year we have seen participants staring at their screens, recording the event through an endless stream of selfies and video footage. Connectivity has come to the playa and a growing number of people upload glossy Instastories, absorbed in themselves, too busy to connect with those around them. It is a sad reflection of what we see in our everyday lives. As in "I, Robot," are we clever enough to anticipate all the consequences of the technology we have built? Can we really deal with what we have created or are we doomed to fall into a trap of our own making?

Pondering these thoughts we spot an enchanting woman, beautifully adorned in a Chinese lantern outfit. We share stories of past Man structures and learn she may have had a hand in creating last year's theme, "Radical Ritual." She shared that she had once told Larry she viewed the Man as her religion, her god, and that Larry had simply smiled and answered, "There is no utopia."

Before heading back, we walk through a giant art installation: a field of lights reacting to movement and sound called *Hexatron*. While utopia does not exist, there are fleeting moments when it is felt. And right now, this is the closest place on earth to it.

The next day I have the heartiest breakfast the playa can provide and it is glorious. Wednesday always marks the point when time seems to start racing like a hot potato and the eccentric encounters start to multiply. I head to a camp which is nothing less than a Burn institution, a long-running bar called Hair of the Dog, or "HOTD," where I indulge in some breakfast vodka shots with my campmates.

Another camp called Costco Soulmate Trading Outlet has been pairing lost souls with their mates for two decades, since 1998. It is a glorious idea that has all the ingenious participation ethics of this wonderous world. We sit around the dusty camp receiving our soulmate pairing training delivered like a game by a sweet man with a giant smile and infectious laugh. Like fully fledged modern-day cupids, we scribble answers on our forms hoping to find Mr. or Mrs. Right, or perhaps a cozy trio. Laughs ring out all around as people open their hearts and unleash their imaginations, sketching out their personalities in the mix of wacky, naughty and spiritual questions.

The true essence of Costco is to act as a lubricant to facilitate connections. Sometimes a little more lube comes from one connection than another. I suddenly find myself baring my soul and the emotions I've lived to a total stranger in the heat of the day while she gives me a cryptic Costco special personality score that will find my soulmate. And really, this is what the playa is all about, and a testament to Costco's longevity.

There are no promises though, and unhappy customers have to brave the (actual) razor fanged mouth of the complaints box if they dare. Clutching my Costco card which will guarantee me a mate tomorrow, I leave satisfied and brimming with enthusiasm. For now, at least.

What better time to go to the camp aptly named Never Sleep Again? Off we go to a stranger's birthday party. The camp proudly displays its wall of shame, snaps of campmates taken when they have sneakily dozed off to sleep. Despite its enticing name, Never Sleep Again is not all it's cracked up to be, and we quickly leave the party to head back to the Brazilian camp. Here it seems a lot of people are actually sleeping.

Exhausted by the rollercoaster of the day I dec12ide to rest and sit with our campmates. Seeking some soul food, I am adamant that I must go to a cacao ceremony that I circled in the guidebook rather than venture out to party with friends, but the Burn has something else in store for me. Another reminder that you cannot always have your cake and eat it.

Instead, roaming the night alone I am caught out in a dust storm. I cycle past the Thunderdome where flesh and leather collide in a cruel duel. Pangs of sadness hit after a flurry of failed connections. The sound stages seem more garish this year, the people more superficial, the magic suddenly gone. The harsh physical discomfort pushes me to my limit.

Once again, I find my anchor in familiarity, heading to the Jazz Café with my partner to soothe away the troubles of the night. It is warm inside, and soulful notes ring out. We meet a cool cat and talk the hours away. Whilst others are raving to mashed up electronic sounds, the playa offers safe havens for all moods, like compact ecosystems you explore to find yourself, to find your people, and the experiences you seek at that very moment. A choice of hundreds of widely different nights in one space, created by those who come together and inhabit the otherwise barren land for one almighty week of the year. Feeling healed inside, I know where to go next.

I see the Temple from afar and my heart begins to expand and soften around the edges. In the dead of night I cycle towards it as it comes more sharply into view, illuminated by a thousand lights creeping up its central arteries, traveling upward to the heavens.

A visit to the Temple should not be undertaken lightly. The moment and mood have to be just right, and it has an uncanny way of calling you when you are ready. In a world of mirth and frivolity it is a grounding presence, gently pulling grief into sharper focus, at once a silent witness to what your heart has to say and an invitation to open up to it.

Parking my bike in front, I make my way silently into it. It is an intricate, monumental structure, spiraling toward the sky in a funnel peak while its base fans outwards, welcoming its devotees through a hundred open doors. The moon perches on the temple's highest peak like a trusted friend, pale and soft in its glow, hiding its tears from the sun.

Pictures of loved ones cover the temple's exposed wooden frame, back-lit by the light filtering in, a hundred eyes watching the world and asking to be remembered. Messages and dedications echo through the space, lingering in our thoughts long after they have been read.

Beyond the words, an energy seems to rise from the earth's core, filtering through the very fibers of the wooden panels, permeating the whole fanlike structure that seems to be softly twisting from a collective and unspoken pain. It travels upwards as the eye is drawn towards the heavens before streaming silently down along the tears that hang from its ceiling. It scarcely seems possible to be here and not feel that energy.

One enters the space hand in hand with the angels and demons we carry, hoping to lay them to rest for a while, seeking solace. The need for a sacred space and shared grieving is deeply etched into the human psyche, yet we have gradually turned away from it, carrying our burdens alone. Today a powerful spiritual undercurrent is emerging in our societies, perhaps a cry to reconnect with the divine, or simply with each other. I leave the space, both heavier and lighter in grief, physical messages and silent prayers remaining. I will return to them later in the week.

Spent, I head to the Dusty Rhino camp to watch the playa sunrise and a special DJ set, but promptly fall asleep laid out on the floor in fake furs before retreating to my camp.

Thursday starts slowly. I let my body rest and recuperate, exhausted from the emotions of the week so far, enjoying a late morning with the camp family sharing stories and laughs. But soon I must prepare again, as today promises a special event, the wedding of a dear childhood friend. The theme of the wedding is white, and I have prepared accordingly.

Playa weddings are always infused with magic, and I have savored each and every one I've been to. A collective purple wedding at AfrikaBurn, a three-way wedding at Fuego Austral, a tear-jerking union at Midburn, my own Burning Man wedding two years before under the wooden vault of the *Sişya* art piece.

The festivities start with a BBQ, and hungry participants shamelessly jostle for space when giant steaks are brought out and tossed on the grill. I stake my turf assertively. I am wearing a self-fashioned crown painted gold, made out of potentially lethal, eye-puncturing wooden skewers, and I am taking no prisoners. There is no wedding etiquette here, not when hot protein is on the menu. The juicy meat is ravenously gobbled, and plates are all but licked clean. There is no gift like a hot meal out in the desert.

I catch up with the blushing bride who is my childhood friend. How phenomenal that we would meet at age 10 and both be destined to attend each other's weddings years later on the playa. We were kindred spirits then and as I look across the crowd, I still see the same light in her face.

Art cars are known as mutant vehicles in Black Rock City, and we board one styled as a ship that will take the wedding party through the dusty "seas." Passers-by wave us off like we are embarking on an ocean voyage. Black Rock City is built on a desert lakebed and aboard the *Christina*, we go back in time to sail its long-ago waters.

All are dressed in white, wing-like floating fabrics and veils catching and playing with the wind, reflective surfaces shimmering against the setting sun. A dust storm brews in the distance. Hot on our tail, it ducks and dives behind artworks in a playful game of hide and seek, giving the scene a dream-like quality, as if the landscape was being painted and rubbed away before our very eyes in a mix between the ethereal seascapes of Turner and an outlandish Dali fantasy. Sublime.

Against the dramatic and changing landscape through which we voyage, the party is in full swing. Light bounces off the sequined outfits and larger than life headpieces of the bride and groom, and the smiles are equally bright. We stop at a suitable "port" and the party steps ashore. Suddenly the dust settles, and everything stands still.

The sun is setting and an iconic art piece is visible in the distance, as if giving its blessing: two lovers locked in an embrace, titled *In Every Lifetime I Will Find You*. The marriage ceremony is led by a shamanic woman full of goodness. She wears two dramatic white horns on her head and her chest is bare. A thick gold belt ties two long and flowing pieces of white material to her waist. She speaks in a calm and accented voice; every inflection is purposeful and full of love.

We hold the bridal path tight between us, a row of gorgeously free souls all decked out in white. And in the end, we come together and form a sacred circle around the bride and groom so we can listen in closely. As the vows are exchanged we bend towards the energy, collectively remembering a thousand loves, hundreds of skipped heart beats, shivers and chills, and a profound deep yearning for another.

I am reminded of why love is worth living for. The shaman's words wake memories dormant inside the heart and head, of a lifetime of loving and heartache, of vulnerability and the beauty of seeing that vulnerability rewarded. Like ships sailing in the night, one will find that safe harbor again and again, and though you are strong and your hand is steady steering alone, the warmth that you feel when a guiding hand covers yours in a storm is worth a thousand circles around the sun unaccompanied.

Now the weekend is upon us, taking us as ever by surprise, and playa FOMO starts to take hold. "Fear of Missing Out" brings a determination to cram as much adventure and goodness as is humanly possible into the next 48 hours. And so begins an almighty binge. What follows will be a stream of consciousness of epic proportions, dipping and soaring like the emotional rollercoaster one eventually finds oneself on when the doors of Brigadoon are about to slam shut for another year.

The day starts with breakfast at the Burn equivalent of the fried chicken outlet. The "Kernel" himself tends to the queue outside, playfully cajoling, making sure his minions are well fed with bourbon and baloney sandwiches. Today my Burn friends and I have declared it Wizard of Oz day, and have coordinated outfits so that we are all characters from the film. I am the Cowardly Lion, decked out in a gold lion playsuit, my tail dragging in the dust. It makes for amusing conversations.

I cycle past a makeshift camp. "Who wants watermelon?" they shout out. As playa serendipity would have it I am carrying a watermelon printed umbrella, which I theatrically open to add to the experience—bam! Play is one of my favorite currencies on the playa. Here, a Burning Man notebook is given as swag in exchange for giving a stranger an inspirational quote.

Next I cycle past a stand where an old dusty Burner is sitting by his lonesome offering spirit animal readings. My spirit animal is the fox, which I am pleased about. My past is the snow owl which I am puzzled about. Moving on I meet up with my friends who are disappointingly not in their Wizard of Oz attire. By this point it is scorching hot outside and this makes a lion very hot indeed.

Realizing the time and the mad schedule I am on, I decide I need to attend a Reiki session on the other side of the city. I have 20 minutes to get there before it ends. This is madness in any world, let alone when it is approaching 104°F outside. Reason does not prevail and I cycle madly on, obviously to be disappointed not to instantly find inner peace in the last five minutes that I attend.

I have to cycle all the way back, making a pit stop at a camel water station. As it so happens, this is by the camp of my soulmate Number One. His camp has a bar at the back, and we talk about our lives, but he is perhaps a little too green, a 21-year-old American, and I have my Wizard of Oz friends to meet and bigger fish to fry. I make a mental note to brave the teeth of the

ONCE UPON A TIME IN THE DUST

complaints box back at the Costco camp about this poor matching. Despite shaky beginnings, this connection would eventually stand the test of time, and I would stay in touch with my soulmate over the years—a true testament to the success of Costco's mysterious matchmaking ways. I would never get the chance to meet soulmate Number Two.

As I cycle back to my Wizard crew over an hour late, I find that they have of course left already. The playa does not wait. I make a pit stop at the camp and find that, happily, our camp neighbors got married during the day. Thirsty for another healthy dose of playa magic I cycle out as fast as my desert-worn legs will take me just in time for the start of the tenth official Burning Man Shabbat dinner, held every year since 2008. With the Midburn experience fresh in my mind, it is one I do not want to miss.

I stop my bike at the Milk + Honey camp, the group holding the Shabbat. I'm ushered to a parking spot in an orderly fashion, the impeccable Israeli logistics manifesting even in this chaotic world. Order is important, as I have arrived at one of the most well attended Burning Man camp events of the week.

Entering the fray, I realize the enormity of this undertaking.

There must be a thousand Burners gathered to take part in this mass ceremony and holy feast. A giant stage has been set up, and coliseum style, people are gathered in a circle around it, bodies pressed together in every space or propped up on the back of the stage as if sitting by the organ choir. Late arrivals shuffle to find a seat, doing so quietly to avoid disturbing the hushed and serene atmosphere.

Behind the stage the sun is starting to set in pastel hues on this most glorious of Fridays. Approaching the circle, I finally spot my adored Wizard of Oz companions and we embrace with emotion, in the knowledge that we are about to witness a thing of beauty together. As I sit with them, we hold hands.

The ceremony then begins. A deep masculine voice rises over the crowd wishing all present a Shabbat Shalom. Our voices ring out and echo as one returning the greeting. Guided by the soothing voice we each take a meditative breath in. All around us chests rise deeply, eyes closed as a rare wave of calm in an otherwise frantic week floods our spirits. On the exhale we are asked to let out a sound. The sound of a thousand breaths resonates around us, reverberating with life.

We are invited to turn to the person beside us to bless the other. Serene faces are turned towards friends and strangers alike offering blessings. Having spent the week connecting on deep levels with strangers in ways that the default world seldom allows, this strikes a chord in all of us. As the service progresses to song, heavily accented Hebrew lyrics ring out, timeless prayers passed through generations. The sun dips behind the stage, now gloriously backlighting the scene. Those who sit in the makeshift organ choir are colored crimson and gold, their tanned legs swinging rhythmically to the music.

As the hushed minutes of chanting draw to a close a woman appears on stage, delivering an impassioned speech that speaks to us all. She talks of the growing disconnect of our societies, rejecting the theme of this year's Burn which glorifies technology, imploring us to instead reconnect with the humanity hot-wired within us, to find solace in each other. She shares a prayer of a disciple who wandered through the desert near starvation, before deciding to give away the first precious mouthful of food, trusting that the universe would provide. "Believe that you too are worthy of a gift," she says.

Her tale ebbs and flows with all the freshness of a mountain spring, her calm and soothing voice honest and pure. The mark of these moments on the soul is indelible; I only wished I had captured each word more fully in my mind.

The ceremony continues to effortlessly weave magic and beauty. Spiritual songs and prayers are interspersed with secular teachings, building a bridge between ancient and modern. Our hearts collectively swell from the love in the air, and we are invited to remember those no longer with us, those we wish could be here, by saying their names out loud. The hand of the master of ceremonies sweeps across the crowd from left to right, and a tidal wave of names are called out in turn, some are shouted loudly, others half-whispered in muted voices, betraying the emotion behind each loss. As hot air mixes with the cooling night, we breathe life into them. Suddenly they are all right here with us. A thousand spirits join the tightly packed circle and we feel the ground under our feet move and the sky stretches us up a little higher.

We are reminded to recognise and hold space for healing. To accept it as part of the human experience, not be afraid to open to it even when it feels like tomorrow will never come. We must also be the source of strength for those in pain. As emotion washes over us, we reach out and instinctively hold the hands of friends and strangers around us, pressing them equally tight.

In a final moment of sharing we all say a word that most accurately defined that day of the week for us. I remember just how intensely we have lived out here as a community. Laughter erupts and people nod in agreement as words like dust or exhaustion are called out. The memories of a thousand souls take us through the week we'd journeyed through together in the city we have collectively built.

As the soulful service draws to a close I see the flushed faces of the people I've connected with during this deeply moving experience. All faiths are present tonight. The message has transcended religions, binding us in a celebration of shared humanity—equal parts joy and pain. As low tables are brought out all sit cross-legged sharing the feast which has been gifted to us, the challah and the wine, and we feel like one family. A thousand strong around the table, a thousand stronger in the sky.

Parting ways, I make my way back to camp. Everything is working magically, and I find those I had lost during the day. We share our recent spiritual experience and learn that out in deep playa the Mayan Warrior was leading its own meditation ceremony. So much wonder at every turn.

The night is young and so are we. My friends and I exit our tents like warriors ready to take on the first night the weekend throws at us. We scoop up some more friends at our first stop and go onwards for a playa bar crawl. Later in the freezing night, we sit huddled and shivering on sofas at an open air cinema bathed in frosty moonlight. We resist sleep, determined to see another sunrise. As the day draws closer we climb up on a platform, finally greeted with a panoramic vision of the playa bathed in pink light. Contemplating the intense week and day I have lived, nostalgia for the city starts to seep in.

Burn night has arrived. I have of course missed all the workshops I had expected to go to; I'll have time to regret those later. For now, a last day of abandon beckons. On arrival, the perimeter around the Man is already thousands of people deep. Nearly the whole population of Black Rock City has gathered to witness it go up in flames. Of all the Burns I would see this year, this is the grail of them all.

The Man Burn is the instigator of the entire Burn movement, from its origins on Baker Beach in San Francisco on the summer solstice in 1986, when a wooden Man sculpture standing at 2.4 meters was burned in a bonfire. The event was co-created and the experience shared with anyone who chose to join, originally organized by Larry Harvey and Jerry James.

The inspiration for burning the effigy was to be an act of "radical self-expression," later to become one of the 10 Principles written by Larry to describe the ethos of the Burning Man event for the new Regional Network in 2004. From these humble roots, the Man has been thought up, erected and burnt to the ground ritually for the last 30+ years. In this year Larry has passed on, making the burning of the Man all the more potent.

Today, Black Rock City has swelled to 80,000 participants, and its Regional arms stretch across the world as a global generation of free thinkers answers the call for radical expression and release.

We park our bikes next to a recognisable landmark in the knowledge that this circle will disperse into the night as soon as the Man topples. As we approach, total madness calls us to it. Mutant vehicles have traveled the desert and crowded around the outer perimeter. A blinding circle of neon lights glares from every nook and cranny, while a jumbled cacophony of music blares out from clashing sound systems. The atmosphere is electric with anticipation.

People pour from all sides of the city to converge at the Man. All are dressed in their finest, outfits and faces glowing brightly, and a million unsynchronized fairy lights flash like a hundred Christmases. The light is surely visible from space. Furry coats flap open, bold patterns and all the costumes one can dream up pop out, proudly exposed to the night.

As people stream in and out, they are walking art works, creativity let loose and radically expressed on a mass scale. The result is like watching the world warped through a giant kaleidoscope. That these people would fall back in line, suited and booted in the default world is almost unimaginable. Why would you stifle such beauty?

Overstimulated by all the sights and sounds, we find a space from which to watch this ritual amongst the people who believe in it so powerfully, countless of whom have seen their lives changed by it forever. Rituals bind us strongly to our ancestors, and the impact of joining a ritual of this scale indelibly makes its mark like a seismic event. The experience of a first Man Burn is etched in the memory of all who have witnessed it.

I cast my mind back to my first sighting of the Man ablaze, a sheet of heat rising from the ground up, awe inspired as flames danced in the eyes and hearts of thousands. It would take me on an epic journey around the world seeking out its warmth far and wide to shake up the status quo, meeting with countless kindred spirits along the way. For this I am eternally grateful.

As we sit in wait a first spark is lit. Audible gasps and cheers break out, all eyes looking straight ahead. Suddenly the whistle of fireworks veering off in all directions pierces the night, propelled into the sky and dramatically exploding overhead. The blue neon lights that have made the Man a beacon in the night are switched off as the fire gains ground, winning the battle. The Man's arms are raised dramatically in the air, surrendering as flames travel up its legs and nest deep in its abdomen. The fire aggressively licks its way up the wooden structure, dominant and blazing all in its path. Within minutes its fiery wrath is inside the Man's head, taunting it with its impending demise. Fire fills the eyes and souls of 80,000, hearts pounding wildly as the structure bursts into a thousand flames.

The Man has guided and watched over us like a spiritual father during the week, our compass, our messiah. Its burning reminds us that everything is temporal, all things will pass, and we must learn to let go. Creating a thing of beauty and burning it to the ground is a powerful and rare statement in our society. It is humbling. There is beauty in the ephemeral, rebirth after death. As the Man finally topples into its fiery grave, the playa roars with life.

The bacchanalia that marks the end of the Man Burn, with participants dancing wildly around its embers, is more muted this year, and the crowds start to disperse, streaming away from the epicenter like a fan. Hot liquid energy pulses through our veins as we ready ourselves by the thousands to go out and conquer the night.

By an incredible stroke of luck, we spot our Oz friends through the crowd and agree to meet under the rainbow later. On our way, we journey to the *Altar of Intentions*, our camp's art structure. The structure was created by a Brazilian team in 2017 and has now received an art grant from Burning Man Project to return to BRC. Last year the team of collaborating architects, light experts, and metal workers spent weeks pre-building it in Northern California. They followed a complex plan to create the beautiful crystalline structure within time and budget constraints. The Altar's side panels are shaped like a torus, an elliptic curve which requires mathematical precision to cut and assemble. The art piece was eventually transported to BRC for assembly on the playa.

The Altar is a vortex of water and a flame will be lit in its center tonight, fire and water converging. It is based on Dr. Emoto's study *The Hidden*

Messages in Water, which proposes that emotional energies and frequencies can change the structure of water, testing the theory through exposing water to different words or music and examining its frozen crystals. The structure invites all to connect with the water through intentions, the water structures later examined and photographed after spending a week surrounded by the energy of the Burn.

After the Burn, the team was astounded to see that the crystal molecules collected in the sample had re-organized into a shape mirroring Black Rock City's layout. They appeared to contain the outline of a central sphere where the Man was placed, and another sphere in the temple's position. It was humbling to be part of a camp offering such a beautiful gift to the playa.

The Altar is just one example of the hundreds of expertly and painstakingly built art pieces, resulting from mammoth collaborative efforts, that go into making this awe-inspiring city, and the Regionals around the world. As my journey ended and I embarked on my own artistic endeavor (as explained in the final chapter), I would realize just how much work went into these labors of love, created for art's sake and gifted to the playa.

Back to the day's events, and after communing with the liquid element, we go back to the Jazz Café, the same place that we found ourselves exactly one year ago at midnight. Entering its warmth and scanning those inside we spot a familiar figure by the bar. None other than Santa. He looks straight out of a Santa casting, decked out in a red outfit, kind smiling eyes, and a hearty stomach. My jaw drops. This is the same Santa I met this time last year in the exact same spot.

Those who have been to the Burn will understand that bumping into someone two years in a row is pure playa serendipity. And this is a decidedly naughty and hilarious Santa. I essentially hijack this man who last year gave me a pair of thigh high socks with a cheeky wink. "The reindeer have been naughty this year," he joked with a deep chuckle. Surely enough, the reindeer on the socks seemed to be mounting each other. This led to various levels of hilarity and made for a memorable playa moment.

As I recount the story to this wonderful man, he reaches into his sack and pulls out a candy cane. "I have another gift for you, but you must promise to share it," he says in a thick American drawl, before adding, "Don't open it till later." I reach out for the candy cane and it immediately drops to the ground. A dildo falls out of the open end and rolls all the way to the bar. Santa's cheeks turn even redder as I retrieve it and we belly laugh until we cry. As if this gift was not enough, Santa then reaches for his saxophone and joins the live jazz band in the Café to the tune of "Santa Claus is Coming to Town." Our eyes light up and we dance like children. They don't call Burn Night 'Christmas' for nothing. We marvel once again at this world that blends epic moments of comedy as the weird and wacky of the planet converge delightfully.

As Picasso famously said, "Art washes away from the soul the dust of everyday life." The Burn infuses the soul with the wonder of so much creativity, gifted by its citizens for others to enjoy, that it makes our everyday lives seem stale and archaic. It is an experiment in collective dreaming, one giant interactive art installation. And we are about to dive headfirst for one last hit of this frenzied fantasy world.

Our Oz friends are also at the Jazz Café and we cycle together to a giant rainbow before lying under a net which coordinates its light show to classical music. It's then onwards to deep playa as electronic music fills the air, assaulting the senses from every corner. The techno gods rule out here, big and dark with ear to ear grins and an insatiable appetite for sounds that make the ground pulse and purr.

I remember that the Vortex of Destiny, a camp I have gone past daily this week, must now be open for business. The vortex is only accessible at night. Eager to cross the long-awaited threshold and finally peer into our destiny, we park our bikes up front. Colors dance and bleed into each other in a psychedelic ocean scene, and multi-colored fish hang from its ceiling. We stand in line and are handed 3D glasses. As we enter, a 3D tunnel opens in front of us and swirls like it's spinning on its axis. This makes us hold the barriers tighter and creep forward slowly while simultaneously merging into this swirling world. It is like entering an impossibly bright Van Gogh painting, and the visual impact is intense, heightened by our euphoric state of mind. Well worth the wait.

Leaving, we pass a roller disco, and I spot a ball pit in the distance. We jump in merrily, colorful balls propelled into the air as we crash into its midst. The playful rules here, every experience urging us to let go of our inhibitions and shatter our preconceptions. This desert playground provides a vital space to release and reconnect to our inner child, so sorely absent in the rigid and compartmentalized default world. A parallel universe of wonder and art that has been magicked up from a blank canvas by its participants. Free from constraints, the imagination is limitless. The dreary and mundane is left at the door. Here the future is lit up in technicolor; once you've seen Oz who wants to go back to Kansas?

We catch a panoramic view of the playa at the Altitude Café, and politely decline the opportunity to be the last five people in the Orgy Dome this year. The night continues relentlessly, and we find ourselves at Opulent Temple, rejoining the reveling crowds, electronic sounds possessing us as hundreds of feet stomp the ground kicking up a (dust) storm. We dance relentlessly, we dance for those who cannot dance, celebrating the gift of movement, the gift of life.

The night's shenanigans draw to an end as the sun rises in the distance. We meet impossibly quirky characters at the temple, pink-wigged and stretched out in yoga poses. A gathering of this scale has brought together all the eccentrics of the world. We are delirious and drunk on the amount of living we have done tonight, mind bent out of shape and rewired to this world of infinite possibilities.

Out in deep playa all of the mutant vehicles are pumping out sounds and raw energy as the entire city roars in unison, celebrating its last night of pure abandon. From afar we see the ubiquitous Robot Heart art car, the brainchild of its much-loved maker Geo, with its instantly recognisable giant wire heart draped with dancers. With the iRobot Man reduced to ashes, we let a new Robot take over. In those moments when dawn breaks and the horizon turns flaming orange, we all sync up to the beat of its heart.

We cycle past Bubbles and Bass before heading back for breakfast at our camp. The city is already starting to pack up, and cars are starting their slow exodus. The Man is no longer guiding us home, and street signs are being taken down as souvenirs, making navigation all the more confusing. Our heads crash out on our dusty pillows, heavy with memories of magic.

Sunday is a day for letting go. The city is now unraveling before our very eyes. All around us camps are being dismantled. The mirth of the previous day is muted, like colors fading from a vibrant fabric. My soul feels heavy, and my body pummeled by dust feels tired. I cycle down streets that have transformed, losing my bearings. The gates of Brigadoon are starting to close.

With time running out, I speed out to catch the last drop of playa sand before it disappears through the giant hourglass of diminishing Burn time. I go on errands which I should have done during the week, when time felt limitless. I do a last trawl, visiting the Burners Without Borders Camp, the Census team which collects vital data on BRC's citizens, and then swing by Regional Burn camps *Gauchos del Fuego* (Argentina) and Milk + Honey (Israel). Later that night I would meet one of the founders of Dragon Burn (China) which would be the impetus for attending my next Burn experience in Japan (although I don't yet know this).

Our own camp is packing up, and contributing to the take-down feel goods, coming together for one final push. A stillness hangs in the air as each reflects on the end of an experience, on the return to the structures of our world. An end of gifting freely, of hugs and smiles. A return to a world of material comfort that paradoxically offers so little comfort for the soul.

Before it all ends there is one final act of ritual ahead of us, collectively letting go of our grief. The sound of a thousand bicycle wheels riding the dust converges in the twilight, headed for the Temple. An eerie mist has risen around us, and dust hangs suspended in the air, a veil above the cracked white earth. As dusk falls, the mist blushes pale pink. I have never witnessed this phenomenon before, and its timing sends a shiver down my spine.

Rising from the mist, *Temple Galaxia* stands before me. Poignantly, it is the final temple design to be selected by Larry Harvey before his passing. As its name suggests it connects our living world to the infinite universe beyond. The physical world that we inhabit is only a tiny element of our reality. The spiritual stretches to infinity, largely-unexplored despite its profound potential to give us key insights into the human condition.

Galaxia is a towering spiral of lattice and an awe-inspiring feat of craftsmanship. But above all it is a labor of love celebrating life, the resilience of the human soul, and those that have crossed into the other realm. It stands majestically in the dimming light, stoic like Jeanne d'Arc awaiting her fate. If the Man is the Burn's founding father, the Temple represents the archetype of its spiritual mother. The devaluation of feminine qualities in our patriarchal culture has led to the mass repression of emotional spheres. *Galaxia* implores us to look inside our hearts, to connect with our emotions and find strength in fragility, providing permission for release.

As night falls the warm lights that line its structure are turned on, flickering in the darkness. Candles lit for each departed soul. A moment of stillness is shared as the crowd communes with the deepest recesses of our minds, making space for the collective catharsis that will ensue. As I observe its delicate frame soon to be reduced to ashes, I remember walking through its inner sanctuary and the whisper of silent prayers. I remember the words etched into the wood, dedications to mothers, fathers, brothers and sisters, children and friends. I recall the faces looking back at me from a hundred pictures. I remember the look on the faces of those mourning, those who now sit together in silent meditation.

Torch bearers crouch low and light one of *Galaxia*'s edges. With incredible speed the fire takes hold, a flash of brilliant oranges, reds and yellows licking the wood dry. It burrows deep inside the lattice-boxed mandala heart, igniting its core. Suddenly cracking erupts from every corner, names released *en masse* into the air. An almighty flame streams out of the open vault like molten lava, filling the night with a thousand spirits.

Those around us take in a sharp breath. The blazing temple is the beating heart of the playa, raw and potent. It cracks with the cries of those that have lost, whether others or oneself. Fiery shockwaves are sent up and down *Galaxia* like a sequence of body blows when one receives news that sends the system into shock mode.

Deep grieving is where emotions are at their most powerful, it is where life, love and pain collide. It provides a portal connecting us to those beyond; as prayers are sent upwards, all our worlds merge: the cycles of birth, life and death locked in an inexorable dance.

Within minutes the structure caves in and howling erupts. The Burn takes one through each stage of grieving, controlled and channeled to begin with, before the fire consumes my soul with such intensity that it opens it right up leaving a gaping hole. One must tear open the whole structure and exorcize all demons to be truly at peace again. The final process of healing is long and slow, as our pain is reduced to embers before the fire finally subsides. There is deep beauty in this process. From the embers the soul emerges more resilient, more balanced, transformed by the lessons it has learnt.

Around us each face tells a tale. The human experience and complexity of its emotional web means we will all have felt pain in varying degrees. Yet we are told to suppress it, to put on a brave face. Here we connect without words, the shared grieving of others taking us in like open arms.

During the week we watched as strangers embraced and cried together, grown men and women putting aside their well-honed coping mechanisms and allowing themselves to weep unashamedly. Seeing this is a balm to the soul when we are so conditioned to shut it out. We live in a world where the individual reigns supreme and strength is glorified, while undesirable emotions like depression and anxiety, byproducts of our broken societies, are brushed under the rug.

To have a sacred space where we can connect with ourselves and with our pain, communing with loss and death, breathes more life into our souls. Here we celebrate every aspect of life, not just the glossy exterior. There is strength in fragility, beauty in tears, light in darkness. *Galaxia* connects us all in prayer, a prayer for humanity.

In its rebalancing of joy and pain, the playa has taught us its final lessons of the week. The temple has provided a vital place to stop and contemplate, meditate and heal. Carl Jung proposed that art can be used to alleviate or contain feelings of trauma, fear, or anxiety and also to repair and restore. It is a dreamlike creation, in recognition that imagery found in dreams helps us find the clarity we need.

We thank and applaud the team of inspirational artists for beautifully orchestrating their intention to "create a space for thousands of participants to have meaningful experiences," to quote their website. The mandala hanging in its core is a spiritual guidance tool. As Carl Jung wrote, "The mandala represents the Self, the wholeness of the personality, emerging during moments of intense personal growth."

By providing both a space and ritual for shared transformation, the Temple has allowed us to connect beyond the individual, to a deep shared unconsciousness with roots in our ancestral and evolutionary past. By tapping into the collective unconscious we can start to unravel the conditioning of modern life which has pulled us away from our "instinctual foundation," disconnecting us from each other and our very nature. Here we can start to heal not just ourselves, but the wounded world around us.

Walking away from the powerful scene, I visit one last sound camp but it does nothing for the soul. I end the night in contemplation, setting my alarm on the dusty phone that has been untouched for most of the week to wake in time for a final sunrise. I have made plans to meet my partner under the rainbow at dawn to watch its final ascent together. I see his silhouette appear, cycling back from a long and eventful Ranger shift, and we smile with love for the other.

In the distance thick pounding electronic music still rings out from all corners of the playa, and we can't help but think they have missed the point. We struggle to find a quiet space to contemplate the last sunrise and take in the awe-inspiring spectacle of raw nature one last time. As modernity encroaches on it, with its glorification of the superficial, it feels like the Burn is starting to lose its essence.

As we pack up and leave, we look forward to a warm shower, a soft bed, but even now we are deeply aware that the briefly lived joy of the material world will be fleeting. We breathe in the playa dust deeply, grateful for the lessons it has taught us while making our final goodbyes.

The harsh desert and hyper-stimulating environment of BRC has a way of stirring up a whole host of emotions. You can simultaneously be having the best night of your life, and be hit by a full scale existentialist crisis. That much living is draining; the midweek meltdown is a real thing. The playa has left me exhausted, disillusioned, in tears, overwhelmed by noise, dust, chaos. For all the wonderful people, there are those you simply don't get on with. Plans invariably fall apart, things break and tempers fray. Just as they can in the default world. Except here you can't close a door and shut the world out.

This year was no different. At this point in my journey, coming back to the Burn where it all began, my expectations were at an all time high. So when the wind (and dust) inevitably hit my sails on those cold and lonely nights, I went straight under. When you've gone all in, disappointment has a particular sting. I had lived and breathed Burning Man for months, putting it all on the line for a rollercoaster seven-stop odyssey around the world. And now I was questioning all the choices that had led me to this decision. What's more I had barely written a word of the book yet. I felt completely and irretrievably in over my head.

In these soul-searching moments everything is magnified. Those around you look like they are having the time of their lives, which just makes you feel more wretched. But the reality is you are facing these challenges with 80,000 other people. Everyone has taken a pilgrimage out of their comfort zone, and is riding the highs and lows of their own waves of heightened living. This is just a natural side effect of immediacy and the growth that accompanies it.

The Vortex of Destiny I had peered into during the week was perhaps a fitting metaphor. I had been assured that it would show me my way, only to come out dizzy and disorientated by its swirling tunnel of flashing colors. The takeaway was simple, there is no clear path or map on the journey of life. When we stop and let that message sink in, any and all paths are valid. Even if it is a yellow brick road.

I realized that if I kept questioning why I had embarked on this trip, I could not relax into it. Rather than leaving everything behind, I had just blurred the lines between my Burn and default worlds. I still had a couple more stops to go, but I was already well underway in the process of internalizing and constructing a new reality—and pursuing something that mattered to me. In time, everything would flow and fall into place.

Like life imitating art, this Lion was finding her courage to fully embrace change.

Chapter 6:
Burning Japan

JAPAN – 5-8 OCTOBER 2018

*F*resh from my BRC experience, I arrive in Tokyo in the black of night, completely disoriented. The following day is spent in a blur visiting the temples of Arasuka, tall and elegant with red slanted roofs, and adorned with pretty golden lanterns. Tourists swarm the area taking photos of each intricately crafted carving while local Japanese girls dressed as geishas teeter past under the shade of pink flowered parasols. The faint scent of incense wafts through the space, and the sound of water trickling down the many water features mixes with the chatter. People wash their hands with long metal ladles before placing offerings to the Gods in little baskets, wishes written on paper notes. This feels like traditional Japan, the one we see in old movies behind the matted shade of bamboo dividers splitting minimalist rooms into microworlds.

Wandering back, narrow alleyways framed by bold Japanese calligraphy signs abruptly make way to surreal nightscapes of skyscrapers and neon. Night falls, and with it jetlag and disorientation amplify. The night lights of Tokyo are overwhelming, with a blue-green glow that comes from mercury vapor lighting. They curve around its bay in a web-like pattern visible from space. The city pulses with frenetic activity and people crowd the streets, barely looking up from their phones behind the anonymity of surgical face masks. The masks seem as much for cutting off unwanted social interaction as for health benefits, and the sea of masked faces make the city look like a gigantic operating room.

That night I meet with the Burning Japan organizer, who takes me out to a local bar. The bar is dark and cramped, filled with people sipping beers in small quiet groups, or on their own. The organizer has been attending Burning Man in Nevada for many years and coordinates the local event on a volunteer basis. She's only able to do this as she doesn't work; managing the organization alongside a high intensity Japanese job would be difficult.

We sit on small stools cradling local beers while she explains the distinctions of setting up a Burn in the Japanese context. For instance, attendees are given wristbands to indicate their consent—or not—to having their picture being taken inside the event. People are very careful about their online presence here due to the extremely formal and hierarchical nature of the workplace—being seen attending an event like Burning Japan could be compromising. As the Japanese rarely take holidays, the event only lasts three days and coincides with a national holiday. That way attendees don't have to take additional time off. This limits the time for immersion, as three days is hardly enough time to disconnect.

During the week that I travel around Japan before the Burn my general impression is of a reserved, polite people, showing few displays of public connection or affection. People seem head-down, absorbed in their own worlds. I stay in one of the capsule hotels in Kyoto, where the individual capsule beds are stacked like coffins complete with a sliding door that shuts out all light. The toiletry products are individually wrapped, and everything is sterile. People barely make eye contact, and everyone keeps to themselves, a very different vibe to other hostels I've stayed in around the world. In these confined spaces, one feels strangely alone despite the proximity to others.

The next day I wander the rainy streets of the Gion district glimpsing temples and quaint alleyways lined with restaurants, doors framed by little curtains. The many restaurants serve beautiful food, pretty as a picture, meticulously presented as art pieces. Restaurants and bars are often full, although most are packed with customers eating alone. People sit alone propped on stools facing the bar, and there is nothing unusual about going to a restaurant unaccompanied. This feels as liberating as it does a symptom of an alienated society. In some places, orders can be made through automated systems, and many stare down at their phones' familiar sterile white glow whilst slurping long soupy noodles without making human contact or looking up.

For the next week, and despite the surface politeness of people, I hardly connect with anyone and sorely feel the lack of eye contact. Of course, this is in part due to the language barrier, but the sense of isolation is somehow deeper than I've experienced in other places. I begin to feel almost invisible. By its absence, I am reminded of how important it is to exchange looks with strangers, to feel that we are seen. I wonder how this will play out in a Burn setting. I recall that in Zulu culture, the word for hello means "I see you," and the response is "I am here." This has a profoundly significant meaning and impact on the foundations of a community. Despite the feeling of isolation, I am surrounded by crowds, and visit sites that seem to cave under the stampede of tourists.

While visiting a bamboo forest, I decide to stray from the beaten path and walk up a road leading steeply upwards to the top of a mountain. The bamboo stretches up vertically, forming an evergreen archway overhead, light filtering through its stems. I walk beyond the forest until the landscape opens up, just as the day starts to set. Nestled in the valley, the surrounding towns are colored sunset pink, and low clouds hang in the air. In Shintoism *kami*, a deity or spirit, is seen as present throughout nature, and it is said that the spirits of ancestors live amongst the clouds. It finally feels peaceful. While the cities of Japan are intense, its nature is sublime.

I travel onwards to Hiroshima, wanting to understand the troubled past Japan has had to navigate, and how this has contributed to the social makeup of its people. Arriving at the memorial standing at nuclear bombing Ground Zero is a sobering moment. The survivors suffered deep physical and emotional wounds. Following the tragedy, services were quickly reestablished through civic effort and volunteers arrived in large numbers to support the effort. This is similar to what took place in the wake of the 2011 Tohoku earthquake. Despite the veneer of disconnection, there is a long culture of sacrifice and solidarity in Japan which resonates with the principles of coming together, volunteering, and building community.

Today Hiroshima is a memorial city and a symbol of peace. As I walk around the Ground Zero site, dozens of Japanese schoolchildren arrive carrying miniature hand-made paper cranes. They set the cranes down on the memorial as a sign of respect for the many children who lost their lives that day, and a silent prayer that this should never happen again. Paper cranes are said to grant Japanese people their wish, and are made in memory of a little girl who contracted the bomb disease—leukemia—a year after the bombings. Following her death a monument was raised as a symbol of hope that no future children would die from atomic bombs. It bears the inscription: This is our Cry, This is our Prayer, That there shall be Peace in the World. The crane is no longer only a Japanese symbol of luck, but a global symbol of peace.

The shift in post-WWII Japanese cultural and aesthetic traditions is reflected in the evolution of Japanese manga and art. Writers such as Takashi Murakami see Japan's surrender and the atomic bombings as the cause of deep scars on Japanese artistic psyche. The country has embraced modernity in an attempt to reinvent itself, due to pressure from both external and internal forces. But doing so seems to have led to a loss of traditions and a breakdown of communities, notably in the big metropolitan cities.

Back in Tokyo I find myself again in the overwhelming hustle and bustle. With a newly met Burn companion in tow, we walk through stores open 24 hours a day, buying different textured individually packaged food. Japanese electronic music blasts from the speakers. It is Friday night and the usually orderly people are out and about, often quite drunk, their usual reserved nature giving way to alcohol-fueled bravado. For the first time in two weeks strangers strike up conversations with me, happy to put their usually hesitant English skills to use.

We are being picked up promptly in a car-share at 6 a.m. to make our way to the Burning Japan site. Our driver nods in a friendly way but shies away from a hug. He does not speak a word of English, so all of our exchanges to coordinate the ride have been via Google translate. Our driver seems to have brought most of the contents of his home in preparation for the three-day event. As we drive towards the event site crammed in the back of the over-packed car, I'm not at all sure what to expect.

From what I have seen so far Japanese culture doesn't seem to have a lot of connection points to the Burner mentality. Formal rules organize life: eye contact is avoided, as is interacting with strangers. Still, people come to Burning Japan to experience connection and disengage from their city lives, putting their ever-present phones away. The event is the smallest I would attend, with only 250 people gathered in a field to live by the principles. Of those 250, a sizable number are expat foreigners looking for connection. A small contingent is Japanese, most very much outside the mainstream.

On arrival the normal hug or roll on the ground for virgins is not offered, but the Japanese Greeters smile warmly. Despite the event's small size, the usual Burn organization has been set up. At the entrance is a makeshift Ranger station, though the uniform is unconventional. One of the Rangers wears a traditional red loincloth complete with Japan Burn logo, his wispy beard braided samurai-style. Burning Japan provides a yearly Ranger training, including background on how Burning Man style Rangering began, how it's integrated into the culture of Burning Man, and what is expected from Burning Japan Rangers.

Following the greeting we walk down the grassy hill carrying what will sustain us over the next few days, and the landscape opens up. The campsite is built in a valley, far away from prying eyes. The setting is beautiful. Rolling hills in shades of autumn, sweetly kissed and turned yellow, rusty and red from the chill in the air. Japanese culture celebrates nature and the turning seasons. The Japanese art of flower arrangement, *ikebana*, focuses on harmony and color use, and as an art form symbolizes their passing. Over the next three days, nature will put on quite a show for us. The leaves change colors daily and flashes of terracotta backdrop this little slice of social experiment.

Scanning the site, I expected elaborate costumes as a reflection of the wild imagination of the Japanese, as in their anime and entertainment. But somehow this playful side is not very apparent in Burning Japan, despite it being a trademark across Burns. After the many maid-cafés and elaborate cosplay costumes on display in Tokyo, this is puzzling. But there are some exceptions to the rule from the more eccentric attendees. One has come to Burning Japan in a gold Egyptian gown accessorized with futuristic glasses. I later find out that he is a professional Pharaoh-for-hire. He does a ninja-style dance for us, and the lightness of the Burn begins.

Despite the lack of costumes, the usually reserved people appear to relax, bend the rules, and escape the beehive of daily life. Here, they are able to connect with themselves and others in a rare informal setting, free from judgment and societal hang-ups. I have not seen so many people smile so genuinely since I arrived in the country.

Given the size of the event, there is little art on show. The 'Man' structure is a Phoenix, small by any Burn standard. It represents money and will be burnt on the second night, symbolically freeing us from materialism. The Temple is majestic, sitting on top of a hill and made of bamboo. Its elegant, delicate structure speaks of Japanese architecture, crafted from natural materials. Spiral shaped wind chimes hang from a colorful vault in its roof, their soft sounds traveling in the cool air. It is covered in lights which shine through gaps in little bamboo baskets.

The Temple is less a place to grieve than the heart of the city. Maybe this is because of the importance of shrines in Japanese life. They are used for keeping sacred objects, not for worship. In this temple, people will leave their most valued possessions, their memories. Like the Japanese wake *tsuya*, a ritual held throughout the night before the day of a funeral, these blessings will "pass the night."

The general setup of the event is small. There is one main dance stage, with three mini trampolines for participants to bounce and dance on in front. The language barrier makes interaction with Japanese attendees challenging, although some speak English, having lived or traveled outside of Japan. Despite the spoken language difficulty, the general body language of people here is more open than what I've experienced so far, which makes a refreshing change. Still there is a noticeable divide between expats and locals at the start of the event, aside from a few mixed couples—usually a Japanese woman and non-Japanese man, rarely the other way around.

After setting up my tent on a slope, I wander the grounds. I meet a wide array of people, including a group dressed up as monks. They are children of American missionaries who grew up in Japan when their parents relocated here. Though they speak flawless Japanese, they are still seen as outsiders given their Western appearance. I am reminded of a situation I saw earlier in the week, when a group of young Japanese schoolchildren on a day trip visibly excluded one of their Western-looking classmates who sat on a bench alone. I wonder if the Burn environment which allows for more open interaction will be able to strip away this ingrained conditioning as the week goes on?

The usual fun and games ensue on the first night in camp. The valley is beautiful but pocketed with surprise ditches hiding thick and gnarly bramble bushes. Once darkness falls, these are like booby traps that disorientated attendees tumble into, to the hilarity of others. The few camps that have been erected have a local flavor. There is an *unagi* bar, its dome covered in lights like a starry night sky. Eel-shaped *unagi* necklaces hang from its ceiling, gifts for those stopping by.

Further up the slope is "Naked Island" and a Japanese sauna. As in traditional Japanese homes shoes are left outside, but here clothing is also optional. The October nights are chilly, and the sauna provides a warm space to while the hours away. Thick steam rises from an opening in the roof, condensing when it mixes with the cold night air. Outside of the Burn event the highly popular saunas and *onsen* baths are part of the local culture, but generally men and women are separated. Here they mingle and chat together, unashamedly naked.

Further afield, a US expat has set up a fortune telling tent complete with a taxidermied weasel she stores in a basket. She explains how isolated she has felt living in Japan as a foreigner, how there is very little warmth in interactions with people, and an all-consuming work ethic. The conformist culture here expects people to work, consume, and generally stay in line; a regimented capitalist system.

The underutilization of mental health services is severe in Japan, as people try to conform to social norms and avoid shame. The word for this feeling of societal pressure is *sekentei*, which translates as "appearance in the eyes of others." The extreme courtesy or *omote* persona, wherein one shows a packaged version of the self dominates, and the ever-narrowing space for genuine interaction is today worsened by social media.

In many ways Burning Man is even more important as an outlet for people living in this environment. Even though the fortune teller was miles from home and had struggled with loneliness, she explained that she came to Burning Japan as here she finally felt like the barriers that separated her from others were relaxed. This is echoed in other conversations I will have with Japanese participants during and after the event. Despite the short duration of Burning Japan, the effects of this new environment do not take long to be felt. Released from stress and societal constraints, the body and mind quickly relax.

The second day at Burning Japan is the equivalent of Burn night, during which both the Phoenix effigy and Temple will be burnt. Given the intimacy of the 250 strong event I already know most of the people here and feel at ease, even though, without alcohol, people seem quieter than on the previous night.

A jam session spontaneously starts up in a neighboring camp. Another camp roasts a whole pig on a spit. Others practice jiu-jitsu or acro-yoga. Of course, the setup is miles away from the megastructures you see at Burning Man. But as I experienced in Argentina, somehow this adds to the accessibility of the event. At Burning Man, setting up an art installation is intimidating and simple art pieces are dwarfed by the sheer immensity of what's on offer.

Here there is space to dip one's toe in creative endeavors however small, and every effort at gifting counts.

One participant has brought a full-size mirror with a single chair in front of it, set up against the leafy backdrop of the hills. He beams at anyone who sits down and looks at themselves in the mirror. It is impossible not to smile back. The message is simple but potent in this country where days earlier I felt almost invisible. It says, *you are seen, you are worthy*. Sometimes the simplest messages say the most, even more so in a place like Japan.

Further down the hill there is a camp with tipi style tents and a huge welcome sign in psychedelic colors. Hugs are given to those who walk past. Again, this simple gesture that we take for granted is very significant in a society where physical detachment of a child by parents generally happens by the time the child enters primary school.

That night Japanese electronic music blasts out of speakers while Burners bounce up and down on the mini trampolines in front of the main stage. Many are wearing anime onesies, grinning like oversize children whilst they fly in the air to the beat. The underground electronic music scene in Japan is dominated by pulsating soundscapes of industrial noise, mixed with recordings of the natural landscapes and sounds.

The DJ has pulled out all the stops with his outfit. Dozens of teddy bears attached to his trouser legs bob up and down as he grooves to the music, little teddy bear eyes reflecting the surrounding LEDs. The Japanese mix with the Westerners, expats of different nationalities including South Africans, Mexicans, Israelis, Americans and Europeans from various countries, the divide between Japanese and the expat seemingly softening as the event unfolds.

On the other stage a strip show is taking place. A Japanese girl dressed in a schoolgirl outfit dances and strips to an audience of exclusively Japanese men. The leering jeers of the men is disconcerting and seems out of place in a generally more progressive Burn context. There are hundreds of gentleman's clubs in Tokyo and a much-mediatized extensive sex underworld. The country has clear gender roles, with Japanese women widely expected to be submissive to men. The submissive role plays out widely in mainstream pornography, and in the highly sexualized depiction of pubescent-looking girls in anime. I walk away feeling a bit uneasy, heading to the Phoenix Burn which is about to start.

As mentioned, the Phoenix is small in size, and its burning happens rather unceremoniously. The Temple Burn gathers a far larger crowd. Japanese fire spinners gather in front of it before the Burn, spinning fire with skilled precision, hypnotically and in perfect unison, the fire leaping and dancing like flaming dragons, casting shadows on their faces and lighting up their dark eyes. They look mystical and enchanting, like Eastern warriors mastering their art, their bodies moving rhythmically to accompany the circular motions.

The Temple is then lit. The fire spreads slowly given the dampness in the air, and we wait for it to take hold in the frigid night for some time. Once the sparks eventually consume the structure it burns brightly, bringing much welcomed warmth. The bamboo crackles, and the delicate panels and hanging baskets are suspended intact in the blazing heat like a flaming mirage. As it burns the many blessings offered to the temple turn to ash and are carried away by the wind, scattering amongst the fertile hills of the valley.

People huddle close in blankets or wrapped up in coats and scarves to keep warm in the autumn night, as the season turns. As in Shinto teachings, we celebrate life together, the passing of time and its seasons reminding us of its magical and inevitable cycles of birth, maturity, death and renewal. In essence, Shintoism is the spirituality of this world and this life, and Buddhism is concerned with the soul and the afterlife. In Japan the two exist together, providing a moral code, a way of living.

Rituals and visits to sacred shrines set the tempo for key life events, including births, the passing of childhood, and the coming of age. The spirits of the ancestors are revered and believed to come down to earth yearly to visit the living. Against the flames of the fire, the social conditioning and anxieties slowly give way to harmony, jogging the residual memory of a time when people joined together to sit surrounded by the *kamis* which exist in nature.

As the temple finally collapses, sparks fill the sky like a thousand lanterns released, carrying our intentions with them.

In the embers of the Temple Burn a huge cuddle-puddle forms, which by some accounts turns into a mass of entwined love-making bodies. In a country where in many settings it is unacceptable to touch a stranger, liberated by this cathartic release people push the boundaries to extremes, seeking out the touch of others.

There is no single place to gather after the Burn. The sound stages are now quiet. Some have gathered in the sauna camp, while others have retreated to their tents. The night grows progressively colder, so I head off to sleep.

The next morning, everyone is already busy packing away as we near the end of this short three-day event, the shortest I would attend, but still filled to the brim with insights and experiences of this quiet land. A young Japanese man with a bejeweled face and feathered hat offers to help me take down my tent. Once packed up I walk round the site saying my goodbyes to groups of Japanese and expats, many now sitting together cross-legged in the field. The social experiment of Burning Japan on Tsumagoi farm was aptly called Sky Island. The event guide describes it in the following words, translated and reproduced in full below:

> *When looking up to the sky, further than the sky itself, you can see a vast floating land between the clouds. This floating land is known under the name SKY ISLAND. The inhabitants populating it have never stepped one foot outside of their motherland, being born on it, living on it and finally ending their lives on it. For them, SKY ISLAND is their only world. The sight that can be admired from this small island is completely different from what can be seen on Earth. There, you can really feel the existence of the sun and the stars. The animals you will encounter on SKY ISLAND seem light and smooth*

both in appearance and in motion. People on SKY ISLAND, cooper-
ate, have high respect and accept each other. You can't live on the SKY
ISLAND by yourself. During these three days, you will become one of
them, being born there, growing and embarking on this exciting trip.

The importance of setting the scene of Burning Japan as almost a fairy-tale, a distant and utopian land, cannot be overstated. It is only when changing the narrative that people who live in a restrictive community can be disinhibited and freed. They are able to embody a new character with a different set of values. Explained in a childlike and playful *kawaii* or cute way they can connect to, as they would with an anime character or in one of the virtual reality games found in the arcades lining Tokyo's streets.

I have seen that by and large the Japanese seem to be more comfortable gifting than receiving, very different from millennials in the West. Some limited their participation to setting up a theme camp or an art piece and spent the rest of the time with little to no interaction. But while not all participants seemed to fully embrace the Burn principles, the growing interactions during the short event felt significant in contrast to daily Japanese life. Unlike the larger desert affairs, here there is no dust and little physical hardship faced; still, escaping from the conformist culture and embracing the values of Sky Island has been no small feat.

One exchange I had with a Japanese Burner following the Burn seemed to sum this up particularly well. He had set up a private area for a meditation space. After the Phoenix and Temple Burns, he decided to remove the walls of the space, to leave the meditation bed under the blue sky. In Japanese culture, the sky is represented in the 5th element *Ku*. Its symbol is the lotus flower, which holds enlightenment in its center. *Ku* is our spirit, our knowing beyond thoughts, and the source of creativity of the world. He described how, in removing the walls, his consciousness changed from himself to others. He spoke of a chemical reaction during the event that freed him from introversion. That this can happen over three days, in a culture that places limitations on the self and avoids interaction with strangers, is a beautiful thing. It is only when we open ourselves up that we can let others in.

Whilst packing up camp I look around at the changed landscape; leaves have turned and thinned on the trees, blanketing the valley from top to bottom in vibrant yellows and oranges. Burning Man provides a canvas for self-expression anywhere in the world. Everyone has the desire to be seen, to feel less alone. This is acutely felt in large cities the world over, and Japanese mega-cities have provided particularly fertile grounds for growing social isolation.

Japanese people traditionally have a deep respect for nature, which has to some extent been lost in the cities they inhabit. The Shinto practice aims to maintain a connection between humans, nature, and *kami*. Here in the valley, it feels like that connection can be rediscovered. Our Japanese speaking driver, who would later tell me of his transformational experience with the meditation tent, waits for us patiently and we leave the site of my first—and infinitely memorable—Asian Burn.

It seems fitting that I should write the Japan Burn chapter in the confined space of an individual hostel pod. This was the most unconventional chapter in my tour of Regional events, living up to what I had imagined it might be. The Burn concepts are largely at odds with the Japanese lifestyle and culture. Taking time out for leisure—radically expressing yourself, opening yourself up to encounters with strangers, hugging and spontaneous physical contact—all of these things seem alien to the way of life here. But it is precisely in these environments that the Burn is so transformative, offering a glimpse of another way. Living in this temporary community helps attendees to see beyond the self, opening up a world of possibilities.

Burning Japan solidified the fact that, just as we need temples for collective healing, we also need frameworks to help us find our voice, communicate and come together. This is especially the case in an environment like Japan. While the people here were more reserved than in other Burns, once they entered a space that encouraged connection, the authenticity of exchanges was all the more striking. Like the Japanese Burner who set up the meditation tent, when the culture around us shifts, a shift gradually happens within ourselves. This is imperceptible at first, until we find that we are ready to take the walls down.

Meanwhile, the intense travel and work schedule I was on was starting to take its toll. Six of the seven Burns I attended that year had been condensed into the first seven months. I was struggling to balance this with remote work across crazy timezones. During the two weeks I was in Japan, I averaged three to four hours of sleep a night due to a combination of jet-lag and work commitments. I walked around in a daze like I was in a scene from Lost in Translation. In a culture where there is an actual word *Karoshi* meaning "death from overwork," I was reaching burnout.

It was only when I took a step back later that year that the magnitude of the journey and its lessons started to come to the fore. Once I quieted the stress and internal chatter that I wasn't good enough, I finally found my voice. After months of writer's block, self-doubt and not knowing where to start, the words came pouring out. It felt like I had finally taken down my own walls.

Chapter 7:
Blazing Swan

AUSTRALIA — 16-23 APRIL 2019

*A*s I plan the final leg of the trip, I start to link up the dots and make sense of it all. I think about my own journey coming full circle in this life adventure. What will this final insight into free living show me? We come to a crossroads in life for a reason and stand peering down the juncture, carrying the baggage of experience with us. The last Burn of this cycle will be in Australia, that vast continent scorched red in the middle and hugged by a coastline of reefs. The last time I set foot there was a quarter of a century ago, a defining year of my childhood, and my head is full of memories of that time.

When touching down, I feel like I've arrived at the end of the world, literally and metaphorically. Perth is one of the most isolated cities on earth, the only city on the entire western stretch of Australia. Even here in its remoteness, it feels just like another city. Perhaps because of this it appears to lack a real identity. The people are friendly in a small town kind of way, and in some ways, it is more a large village than a town, though the same shopping chains that can be found everywhere in this globalized world are here too. Though far from the big cities of Australia's Southeast, it feels equally far from the rugged authenticity of the outback.

It's difficult to find the outback's authenticity until you scratch the surface of these big concrete jungles and get your fingernails dirty with Bogan culture. Bogans are Australia's rednecks, and maybe twice as rowdy. If there was a Bogan vs Redneck beer-off, the redneck would end up passed out under a table or in the cargo area of a ute—the ubiquitous Australian pick-up trucks—first. Not surprising that the Mad Max world—which the Burn is often compared to—is set in a post-apocalypse Australia.

Visiting Coober Pedy, the set of one of those films, is downright bizarre. The town emerges out of nowhere on what seems like an abandoned high-way that goes on for miles and miles, halfway through the long desert road between Adelaide and mystical Ayers Rock. A desolate settlement that gets hot as hell, and where people literally have to burrow underground to survive. In the local Aboriginal dialect, 'Coober Pedy' means "White Man in a Hole." Half of the city lives in deep dug-out opal mines. It takes a particular character to live here.

We wind through the orderly Perth suburbs until we reach the remote town of Kulin, where Blazing Swan takes place. Flat farmland framed with gum trees rushes past us as I sip on a most delicious rum in honor of my journey's end. There are "Danger Kangaroo" signs up everywhere, much to my delight as a foreigner. My car mate is of Polish descent. We chatter throughout the four-hour journey and, as tends to happen when sitting next to a stranger for an extended road trip, end up telling each other our life stories. Well at least the highlights that have defined us.

I quiz him about what being from Perth means and what the culture there is like. As it turns out the Perth identity isn't straightforward. It's a mosaic of people from all over Europe congregating in one city. But what pulled these people to travel to the middle of nowhere and set up shop in the world's most isolated city? Mining it seems.

The mines in Western Australia define the people, who make a healthy living by extracting the gold and iron underground. The very soil that we grind under our wheels is heaving with it. Job opportunities for the young men here are mostly in the mines, and the work rotation means they are away from home a lot of the time. Because of this, drugs and alcoholism have become a serious issue in this part of Australia. All of this puts strains on families and has created a culture that loves to party hard. For some the Burn is just another *doof*—or bush party, than an exercise in living the Burn principles.

The Blaze organization is supported by the City of Fremantle, aka Freo, the hippy epicenter of Perth. Their 900 square meter warehouse headquarters, otherwise known as The Nest, is also located in Freo. The Burn here hosts around 3,000 people and has been running for five years. Due to competing sound camps, issues within and between organizing groups were rife this year. Perhaps this is just a reflection of the mindset that develops when a community is isolated. But the Burners here also have a no-bullshit, down-to-earth mentality, which one has to admire.

We pull up to the Blaze gates in the Kulin desert at sunset, and are welcomed by Bird Man, a cockatoo on his shoulder. Abode, our camp, is in full build mode, and we join in as the sun goes down.

The camp is one of the largest at Blaze, and its infrastructure has been meticulously planned over months. The camp meals are also prepared by different kitchen teams in Perth so they can be more easily prepared on site. I would join my team for fun days of cooking and camp planning before heading out. I also created a fairy inspired space, where I would gift readings.

Even though build is still underway, the partying starts in earnest that same night to celebrate our new home. We meet colorful characters galore in the neighboring Treetops Camp. Huddled together in a truck, we chat the hours away as the world blurs around alcohol-soaked edges, puffs of smoke swirling into thick intoxicating clouds in the confined space. I am wedged between a man in a large, feathered hat and a dark-haired goth dressed head to toe in black. So many conversations that I wish I had captured in that warped first night. We stumble back to the tent and despite my fear of spiders and particularly thorny plants that grow onsite, I cross half the camp barefoot and crash out in the tent on a deflated mattress.

I wake in a dehydrated heap. The next day we continue working on camp build, hoisting the marquee together in an ad hoc way whilst pesky bush flies try to get into every crevice of our faces. Relentless.

Half the population here seems to work in manual labor, and the electricians and construction workers of the camp provide some direction in the chaos of set up. It is a far cry from the organized precision of Midburn, but all done in good humor. The marquee is decked out with a ridiculously powerful sound system for the loudest of tunage. It can probably fit about 500 party fiends, and is filled with psychedelic paintings that react to UV lights and decorations made by the camp. These would get interesting later.

I take a break to attend the welcome ceremony, and a member of the Department of Public Works (DPW) barks out orders. "Get out of your theme camp crew and meet a stranger!" We dart through the crowd, hugging throngs of unknown bodies to set the tone for the week. We are then walked through each Principle in turn, with eyes closed like a guided meditation. This collective bonding moment would be one of the few organized during the week. The effigy lays on its side behind us. It is Larry Harvey's famous hat in an ode to this year's theme, Happy as Larry, and is framed by two slightly odd-looking swans.

Theme camps are finalizing their setups and crowds of attendees are arriving as the gates officially open. The site is built on a hill, flanked by tall majestic rocks that unsteady Burners would clamber upon nightly to see the sunset, with dry shrubs with gnarly looking spiked arms dotted here and there, and tall gumtrees catching the wind dreamily in the distance. A salt lake rests on one side, white and still, its multitude of textures lying in wait to be explored, baking under the midday sun, the white dusty bowl shape conjuring up memories of the Burning Man playa.

Our camp has a nightly theme and the opening bash is White Wednesday. We all follow suit and deck ourselves out in bonkers white accessories. An art car called Champagne Charlie appears to whisk us away and give us the tour. We climb onto collective "woops" and "yewwws!" Champagne Charlie meanders through the event site, and happy faces wave and smile at us all along the way. We stop as people clamber onboard to join in the celebration, euphorically welcoming the week ahead. The theme camps have all sprung up and are open for business as the sun sets on this opening night.

Sound Alley is the most populated part of town. Once again playfulness is the name of the game and its diversity reminds us that the human imagination knows no limits when allowed to run amok. Lining the streets are diverse sound camps such as a life-sized Star Wars starship, a gigantic bird nest dome, a towering sound tree complete with side dog kennel for when you need to be sent to the doghouse (mostly willingly), and a massive Egyptian pyramid. We are once again immersed in a landscape that's like a George Lucas acid trip meets Mars.

More so than other Burns, the party is the main event at Blaze and the sound camps rule supreme. Sound Camp Alley never sleeps. Night and day it is rocked by deep powerful sound systems, bigger and bolder each year. It is a battle of the egos with each camp cranking up the volume to impossible decibels despite the modest space they occupy as if straining to outdo the other. Drum and Bass and Psytrance dominate the scene, sending the heart into arrhythmia. With the relentless sound filling the ears, and the body possessed by the penetrating pulse of the bass, the mind just stops thinking.

Everyone moves together in this trance-like state: disconnecting on a mass scale. All that exists is the music, this moment, the night, and whatever is coursing through the veins. People amplify their present state, elevating it through an intoxicating cocktail of sound and hyper-stimulation as serotonin levels hit the roof. Trying to sleep in a tent with these audio levels requires serious exhaustion, and I would do everything in my radical self-reliance power to find other sleeping arrangements during the week.

Many Blaze-goers will not leave this madness all week, pushing the sleep deprived body to new levels, reflecting the doof movement. In Perth, every other person is an aspiring DJ and Blaze is used as a platform to promote one's new tunes and record label. This type of self-promotion feels at odds with the Principles, but that seems to have been overlooked.

As the most isolated town in the world, the Perth community is tight, and many attendees know each other from home. This gives another feel to the Burn as many do not venture far from their comfort zones, mixing with their friends and following a set agenda to make sure they catch each other's various performances. Here it is hard to wander off for a night of anonymous exploration without bumping into someone you know from your circle, even people you work with. The impact this must have on radical self-expression and the feeling of disconnecting is huge. Still, the closeness of the group helps with cohesion.

Further afield camps provide other eclectic experiences: a costume camp, a bar comically guarded by a blow-up crocodile, a church of belligerence, an art gallery with a mechanical horse that poops Mars Bars and tripped out visuals—ingeniously named Freakwhensee.

And then some peace. Infinite Loop rests on top of the hill for chill times. Those looking for downtime flock to it. In the middle of the hecticness that is Blaze, it welcomes you with soft and dreamy arms. It is like a fairy-run world, all soft lights and billowing trees with camps where the floors are lined with carpets, pillows and quilted blankets.

In these cozy surroundings we sip tea served out of giant iron dispensers and recoup while talking with strangers. I meet a man in his 60s with round glasses and a funny hat. One of the gifts of the Burn is that it gives us these little golden moments where we can meet people across all age groups. Nowadays, aside from our families, we tend to have limited interaction with older generations, and few role models who have kept living freely outside the limits of society well past the age where you're supposed to settle down and grow up.

The neighboring camp to the tea house is the Dream Gallery. We hang out for a while in its suspended nets stretched out like beds that you have to climb up to like an acrobat. It feels nice to be up in the air and watch the world underneath through the netting. In each net is a little microcosm of social interaction. Some are chattering in groups, others are resting a while, their arms crossed over their chests, sound asleep like napping children.

Outside it is bitterly cold and everyone is decked out in highly cuddleable furs and onesies. It's like one big zoo has gathered in this Dream

Gallery world, fluffy zebras, leopards and human-sized unicorns laze around. On my way back to camp I pass an installation called *The Whisper Tree*, an Australian gum tree all aglow with colored LEDs pulsating in time with each voice that passes it. During the day, it plays a different sound to you, creating worlds of sound through tiny round speakers, floating suspended on long wires that catch the wind like branches of a willow tree.

Thursday is for exploring. I stand in line for coffee and steampunk pancakes, always a great opportunity to start chatting to the costumed strangers-soon-to-be-legends lined up next to me. A woman is there with her three-year-old daughter. "Has it been difficult for you here with the little one?" I ask. She tells me with a smile that no, it's been a relief. "Usually she takes up all my time and energy but here everyone plays with her." I think about how true that must be. When children aren't raised in communities the strain of raising them falls completely on their parents. And how socially stunted we must be as a result, in such narrow social circles.

After coffee and pancakes we head to a jostling tournament at the Church of Belligerence—as you do. Nutters dressed in medieval outfits club each other before a riled-up crowd. Next up is an eye-gazing workshop but when I check it out it's just people lounging around chatting, so I head to the Temple to take stock and reflect.

The Temple at Blaze sits on top of a hill, wood-carved in a lotus shape, a light and airy space to wander through. A man has set up in one of the far corners, playing rhythmic music on a violin. There's a beautiful echo, bouncing off the wooden panels covered in messages full of intention. Getting up close to the panels, some look blackened by smoke as if the imprint of flames was already etched on the wood.

I sit down on a bench and take off my boots, pressing my feet to the ground. I think of my journey and where it has taken me; after all this will be the last temple of my seven Burns. I close my eyes to try to find clarity. Suddenly the music stops and all that is left is the rustling of the wind through the wooden structure, a dramatic pause in the script. The warm autumn air feels thick with silence. It's moments like this that seem to bring meaning to all the madness, like silent messages from above. Before I leave, I write a note on one of the panels, purposefully the only one I've written in all of the Burns I've traveled to this year, as a way to mark the end of the tour. It was not about arriving; it was always about the journey itself.

That night the full moon rises; a giant orb over the stillness of the white salt lake. It is majestic, round and full, beaming so strongly that it lights up the smooth bed of the lake, which glows eerily and reflects it. Groups of people around me gather to watch its steady rise, from blood orange to radiant white, and we smile at each other. They say the southern hemisphere's sky is even more eye-catching than the northern view due to the Milky Way's bright central area rising overhead. It's not often that we celebrate nature. I can't help thinking that memories of our animal spirits must still sleep within us as they seem to stir when we enter the wilderness. There is no better moment to go and explore the David Attenborough Greenhouse—a giant of the natural world.

We enter the Greenhouse dedicated to this legend of a man: a green dome covered in artifacts celebrating his life, and filled with plants. In the back is a shrine with a picture of the man in a wooden frame, holding a tiny green frog and smiling with goodness. The grandfather of nature study himself. I'd be back here two days later, by chance with a girl whose grandfather knew Attenborough personally. With emotion she explained to us how her parents had waited till her 18th birthday to give her an autographed copy of one of his books. By the time she opened it, her own grandfather had already passed.

As she tells us the story, someone at the back shouts out for her to "Put your hand in the bowl of water and touch one of the plants with your other hand." As she does the whole space lights up, and with every plant a different recording of Attenborough's familiar voice, and the sound of tropical animals are activated by the electrical circuit created.

Here, in the middle of the barren Kulin desert, we are transported to lush rainforests and mountain peaks as memories of epic planetary land-scapes jolt to life. Every heart in the space is warmed. To think this man and all his wisdom could soon disappear at a time when we need his teachings the most. May we collectively continue his life work, long after he is gone. It's hard to imagine an experience could live up to the Attenborough legend, but the people behind this camp nailed it. We walk down the hill beaming and doing our best impersonations, narrating the world around us Attenborough style.

Back in party-town I dance joyfully with all the good vibes amassed that day. Standing by a fire pit with the *Treetops* crew, enjoying top-class banter and a delicious beverage from a beautiful Game of Thrones-esque goblet. It is poured from a giant horn—hence its name: Horny Juice. To this day, I do not know the recipe for that elixir.

"Put your hands up, stay right there!" someone shouts at us from out of the blue, then runs forward and wraps security tape around us before declaring the area a danger zone. Being too hot to handle is the crime. We fall around laughing, then migrate to the camps which are like different universes of sound that we bounce to, heaving with people decked out in lights and decorations like glorious Christmas trees. Totally spent, we retreat back to camp and sit in sofas for hours, huddled for warmth, laughing the night away with a vast choice of epic characters including a Jesus and an Ali G lookalike.

Following suit with other events, and to honor the indigenous community, a Welcome to Country ceremony is organized the next day. Welcome to

Country is a speech delivered by an Aboriginal elder acknowledging the traditional owners of the land past. The ceremony kicks off with two men sitting side by side playing didgeridoos. They are totally focused on their art, inhaling and exhaling deeply as throaty sounds expand outwards from their abdomens in vibrating waves. The long instruments are decorated with traditional artwork and the musicians rest against a painted mural with a rising sun in its center.

A traditional fire is then lit in iron barrels, thick plumes of smoke quickly rising and filling the air with an aromatic smoky eucalyptus scent. This smoking is believed to have cleansing properties and the ability to ward off bad spirits from the people and the land. Mainstream Australians are still largely segregated from Aboriginals, and the two cultures seem to co-exist uncomfortably together. Even if the ceremony is a token gesture, it feels good to experience a moment where that's not the case.

Given the Burn principle of Radical Inclusion, it's surprising to see how little Blaze incorporates indigenous expression, when the artwork of these communities tells us so much about the country. These artists are great innovators, drawing on deep cultural knowledge and using an abstract artistic language which opens the mind to new ways of seeing. Dot paintings narrate creation stories or map tracts of land. They are tangled with energy and flowing movement, sweeping inky pathways linked together, and softly dotted, connected rings evoking a landscape of hidden waterholes. Structured branches and pathways criss-cross like a mind map of the red bush, the brushstrokes of fine ochre inviting us to retrace ancestral paths.

Today the Australian land, like much of our earth, is sick. A hole sits in the atmosphere here, and its famous barrier reef is being aggressively bleached. The latest election, dubbed the Climate Change Election, ended in climate change denialists holding on to power.

The indigenous Aboriginal people have cared for and respected this land for generations, thriving in its desert center. They hold knowledge of the watercourses and locations of rock holes. In their oral language there is a word to describe the relationship to the land—*Wapar*—which also encompasses Aboriginal law and religion. All features of the land have names and are related to a story. The past and present are part of the same thing, a continuum—total immediacy because time is irrelevant.

We have much to learn from these ways of living, built with nature at their center, though the Aboriginal voices have been largely silenced. Their beautiful story of creation honoring the land goes like this:

> Is this a dreaming world? The Earth was a flat surface, in darkness. A dead, silent world. Unknown forms of life were asleep, below the surface of the land. Then the supernatural Ancestor Beings broke through the crust of the earth from below, with tumultuous force.
>
> The sun rose out of the ground. The land received light for the first time. The supernatural Beings, or Totemic Ancestors, resembled creatures or plants, and were half human. They moved across the barren surface of the world. They traveled, hunted, and fought, and changed the form of the land. In their journeys, they created the landscape, the mountains, the rivers, the trees, waterholes, plains and sandhill. They made the natural elements: water, air, fire. They made all the celestial bodies: the sun, the moon and the stars. Then, wearied from all their activity, the mythical creatures sank back into the earth and returned to their state of sleep.

The sun begins to set behind the hill, lighting up this ancestral scene of smoking fire and storytelling, bouncing off the tilted effigy. We walk away feeling a little bit lighter after paying our respects to the elders who conducted the ceremony. Heading back to camp we hear the music start up again in the sound camps, in total contrast to what we have just witnessed.

I put on my furs to join the Friday night madness. The night air is freezing, and an almighty storm begins to brew. We jump over barriers to a pop-up cocktail bar and shuffle to the pounding music, but tonight the lights seem too bright, almost garish. The feeling of being out of place is accentuated when you're tired and miles from home. It feels like people here prefer to stay within their social groups and don't step out of their comfort zone, perhaps an inevitable feature of small-town mentality. It's time for an early night and I pass out in the van blissfully unaware of the storm raging outside.

The next day dawns still and I wonder what the fuss was all about. Walking round to the main camp area I see that the whole side of the marquee has been uprooted and destroyed, the metal bent double by the force of the wind. Jaffled. If it hadn't been for the comfort of the van, I'd have spent the night wrestling with my tent to stop it from being flattened. The whole of Blaze is like a battlefield, camps blown over, tents destroyed. In the midst of this chaos, people from neighboring camps come by to help out, and someone wheels in a mobile cart of steaming hot food as we rally together to rebuild our city; all is back in order before nightfall.

Saturday night then rolls in. Tonight, the effigy will be burnt, and mayhem will erupt. We go to it like moths to a flame. The effigy this year is smaller than other years, I am told. A few years ago, a giant swan was built and burnt so greatly that it set a neighboring camp on fire. This year Larry's Hat has been put up with less fanfare, flanked by the somewhat comical looking swans.

The speed with which the structure takes flame is breathtaking and it feels like the whole ceremony is over before it's even started. There is little time for reflection, unlike at other Burns I've experienced where one follows the gradual fall of the structure in reverence. Here Larry's iconic cowboy hat—mythologized in Burn circles—is reduced to flames and collapses in minutes. It finally feels warm out in the cold night air and a few brave people strip off to dance around the smoldering remnants of the effigy, pagan style.

By this time all the camps are pumping with music and heaving with carnivalesque people. The smiles are as big as the beats. We dance with giant jellyfish, losing ourselves in those moments when the music takes control and moves your body to its every whim, each electronic pulse sending a shockwave to the brain until you become one with it, burrowing deep into those primitive urges for wildness. Nothing exists but the bass, colors, lights and the vibration of a thousand feet hitting the ground while arms are thrown up to cut shapes in the air.

In this madness, you can catch someone's eye and move together without needing to say a word, collectively rocked and transported by the music. The soul leaves the body for a bit in this trance-like state, teetering on the edge of insanity. The music electrifies the crowd, and as one after another tribal beat is dropped we answer its call, howling through the night like a pack. This is what Blaze does best.

We move with the crowds and eventually find ourselves, appropriately, in the doghouse. A dog kennel built by the Treetops Camp and one of my favorite spots in Blaze. It's packed full of teddy bears and lit by UV reflective lights. As we bury ourselves in this mangled fluffy mess a man enters the fray. His face is completely decked out in UV paint with the same leopard spot pattern as the kennel, perfectly camouflaged and glowing.

And then time stops. So many artists and wonderful minds are gathered at the Burn and I am about to have my mind blown. Amongst the teddy bears I am handed a gift, a rolled-up painting. As I unroll it slowly a dreamscape comes to life. I am sucked in as it unravels. My world at once narrows and expands to take it in and make sense of it.

The complexity of the detail feels like diving into layers of consciousness, staring into a looking glass where the twisted mind of the artist curls the edges. They don't say 'the devil's in the details' for nothing. Darkness of the soul lays on one side, tricksters lurking in the weeds, the depths of the forest heavy with primal urges hiding in the undergrowth. The challenges we must face lie in the middle, adrift on an island that seems to sprout from the land and speak in elvish tongues. And all the light at the other end. A spiraling path leads us upwards to the gates of enlightenment, if we let the universe provide. Onward toward the kingdom of the sun.

In the end, we all walk the thin line between sanity and madness, movement and stillness, joy and pain. The darkness pulls us away from the light, but we somehow know that we will make our way back to it, in an endless senseless cycle. The Burn lets us crack all emotions open in full glory: the moments of niggling self-doubt, the weirdness that makes us feel alive, the times of almost superhuman power when we feel elevated to a higher plane. The wretchedness and the sublime. The whole human experience amplified, if we dare to live it.

I finally pull away from the scene. I swear I have seen this land in a dream before, and right now it glows in my lap as if drenched in ethereal moonlight under the UV lights. Art is to be experienced, and when it strikes a chord, it's because you are feeling the soul of the person who created it. Although the whole picture has been drawn in gray pencil strokes, I see it in hyper-color.

The rest of the night rushes past in a whirlwind. We sit beside a giant pulsating heart attached to a rib cage and challenge all coming by to find a song with the word "heart." The cold interrupts our fun, and we have to do some serious acrobatics and balancing acts to get out of furs and onesies, ridiculous trinkets and fairy lights when in the porta-potty. One of the most dreaded Burn moments. After some more dancing in the bird nest we go to sleep in the tea house under a pile of blankets.

The great salt lake lays before us like a mirage under the brutal midday sun. With my campmates in tow, we go to it like a band of merry men. People dance on the dry riverbed, a vision of gold and silver wings catching the light, colorful patterns, and some eccentric wearing a full-on scuba outfit complete with fins. As we head inwards towards the middle of the lake, we enter different worlds of textures. The sandy shore turns to sticky mud before drying to crunchy salt patches underfoot. The music fades into the distance as we move further away, and the dancing crowds become small flecks of silver and gold against the lunar landscape. It's a beautiful day, and in the distance the trees lining the sandy "coast" look strangely like palm trees lining a pristine, exotic white beach. The glare of the white salt bed is blinding as we make our way back, but the warmth of the dipping sun on my skin feels amazing.

We gather on the hilltop at sunset and get ready, connecting with memories tugging at the heartstrings. The Temple Burn always brings up emotions. The fact that this is my last one on my Regional journey adds to my need to feel. The fire is lit, and the lotus starts to crackle with the first sparks. We gather to honor those who have passed through our lives and into the next, and to burn down the old in ourselves and bring in the new.

Fire is a life-giving force on Australian land, as I would learn later on my road trip. Driving into the country's center is a journey of epic proportions. Endless Australian outback rushes past in a sea of primary colors. The deep red of the soil, vibrant yellow of the dehydrated grass, green of the shrubs and gum tree leaves, all against the blue sky.

Looking at the gum trees, I find myself wondering why their white bark is splashed black here and there. The Aborigines carried out mosaic burning for biodiversity, and the whole ecosystem is fire dependent. The rangers periodically light the national parks on fire and this burns the trunks of the trees black, but the rest survives. Burning is part of the land regrowth system, a symbol of renewal. Just as fire gives nature a second wind, it stirs emotions within us.

I think of the outline of flames I saw etched on the wood, already marked by their destiny, when I visited the Temple earlier in the week. Death is imprinted on all living beings, and we move towards it in time. Like the Australian national emblem, the emu, we can only move forward, not back. In "Dreamtime" an individual's entire ancestry exists as one, we are but part of a continuum. The Aboriginals performed ritual ceremonies and customary songs near sacred sites to please the ancestral spirits and to keep themselves alive. In a time and culture where there are few ceremonies and rituals left, we feel a pull to do the same. The Temple fire rages in the distance, an open portal for the spirits to rush through.

After this emotional catharsis the city starts to wind down. The final flurry of workshops have taken place this week, with highlights like Bogan yoga. We hang out at the comically named God Said No Camp (GSN). This was the first ever camp at Blaze and was baptized GSN after a conversation with the landowner when they were scouting an event site. The owner changed her mind about leasing the space at the last minute because "God said no."

Later, I appropriately hang out with Jesus to watch the last sunset on top of the rocks. Up on the rocks we share stories that have affected us deeply. There is a story behind his choice of outfit. He is dressed as Jesus as his Mary tragically passed away early this year. They met at last year's Blaze and fell in love, making a pact to dress like Jesus and Mary if they came back. But now he flies the flag alone. Jesus without his Mary but with a giant size heart and shoulders to carry her here.

As the sun sets in the distance the clouds form tall shapes, as if playing out the story in the sky.

That night I sleep alone in my tent on top of the hill. The sun is starting to rise as I go lie down. Two hours later I'm up, packing all my things while

ONCE UPON A TIME IN THE DUST

the campground is dismantled around me. My mind is a blur of exhaustion, working through thoughts of this week that is drawing to an end.

As serendipity would have it, a Beatles song that I listened to as a child 25 years ago on this very continent starts to play in the distance, like a message from the universe signaling the end of the journey. The chords ring out and grab me by the pit of the stomach, blue with nostalgia. Each note is a layer of memory that elevates to the tip of the present moment, while past and future play out in the mind's theater below.

A jumble of memories and hopes collide in complex wavelengths, like the dispersion of light through a prism, and I freefall between them, darting up and crashing down through a richly layered daydream. All the moments experienced over a lifetime seem to have been leading up to the now, and suddenly I understand that I'm where I should have been all along, in a place where I feel alive. There is no end to the journey. Just keys of experience with which to unlock new doors.

The lyrics ring out beautiful and achingly full of meaning. People say that what we are seeking is the meaning of life, but we are actually seeking the experience of being alive. All the colors of nature around us seem enhanced when we take the time to see them. Love is within and around us when we stop to realize it. Tears sting my eyes and my heart swells as I look up at the sky. The moment over, I walk down to help pack up the camp.

This final night, the camps join for a last dinner. We all bring dishes and sit down to talk together. It feels like the perfect end to the journey, the make-be-lieve world stripped down to the simple one of interaction. Around the table, we collect passages of joy. All the tired faces gathered around haven't washed in a week and look just a little wild, but so happy. That happiness that you get when you've spent a week bent out of shape, but have somehow bent back into yourself.

Here as in all the Burns, behind the veneer of bravado that Australian people often put on, people come to find healing and connection. Broken families, substance abuse, domestic violence, and a sense of disconnection seem to affect this isolated part of Australia. I work through some of the conversations of the week: the bodybuilder hiding his insecurities behind an ultra-masculine exterior, the group comedy act working through a year of blows, people living life uprooted on the road. All have the same yearning for belonging on this rocky journey of life.

Maybe the Burn is less about getting out of your comfort zone than it is about finding your comfort zone. In the months to follow, the emotions I lived through would retreat like the tide, leaving an indelible imprint as they did. What I had experienced was a unique place in time, where people from all corners of the world signed up to ideals that they struggled to find in the empty spaces of our modern world. Some of them came out changed, with the stamp of a new tribe deep within, and ready to take the learnings out to the default world.

As I drove away from Blaze with one of my campmates, the power of the final Temple I had experienced and found the strength to write in, and the tragic story shared by the Burner dressed as Jesus resonated in my heart. I finally felt compelled to confide in her and disclose the deep loss of a close family member that I had experienced as a child. It is one that I am still struggling to process and come to terms with; the protective layers built up from years of carefully bottling up emotions are hard to peel away.

I thought back to the child I was 25 years ago, confused and still battling to make sense of this loss on this very continent. Perhaps this journey had been just as much about putting those demons to rest and finding a way to channel grief.

The physical journey was over but the lessons of its highs and lows continued to crystallize. Some months later, as I stood in the kitchen chatting with my sister, I worked up the courage to bring up the painful memories of the past. For the first time we spoke openly about our shared loss. I felt my soul breathe a little lighter.

To mark the end of my journey around Burns, I put together a small art project to honor the temples of the world, and their incredible power for healing and transformation—not least my own. In the words of Khalil Gibran, "The deeper the sorrow carves into your soul, the more joy it can contain." Each Regional Burn applies its own significance to the temple in line with its beliefs. For some, it is a space for shared grieving, a symbol for finding one's own path, or a place for renewal. For others, its absence speaks volume of how a culture suppresses grieving and the spiritual world.

The art piece included pictures of temples from each of the events I had attended, as well as audio recordings of passages describing these spaces read out in local voices. Poignantly, my father helped with the project turning some of the pictures I had taken into beautiful paintings. He had been the glue that held our tight-knit family together through difficult times, and his gift moved me deeply.

I placed the art piece in the 2019 *Temple of Direction* at BRC with the help of the Temple Guardians. At different points I went to see how participants interacted with it. Some stopped to look at the pictures and listen to the audio through the bunny-eared headphones before entering the space. Others interacted with it after experiencing the temple, with tears still in their eyes. Some left messages of gratitude. One message read: "What a powerful project. Thank you for illuminating the global community. I'm so glad the temples are similar, yet representative of their cultures. Your work made me feel connected to the whole world in our shared grief and joy."

This was precisely the message I had tried to convey.

As I watched the *Temple of Direction* burn, exorcizing our collective grief and celebrating our strength against adversity, I thanked it for helping me on my journey. Little did I know then that this would be the last Burn to take place for two years, and that soon we would need its temples and spaces to commune more than ever.

Chapter 8:
A Time of Not Burning

LOCKDOWN – 2020

*I*n 2020, the world was abruptly put on hold in a way that we could not have imagined, affecting communities globally and changing the way we gather. Thanks to the COVID pandemic, Black Rock City and most of the Burning Man Regional events were canceled for the first time in Burning Man's history. Likewise most of the other human gatherings so eagerly anticipated during the long summer months, those times when we come together for celebration, as it feels so natural for humans to do. This year is different, almost surreal. With the world on hold we're separated from others, socially distanced and navigating alone through times of great uncertainty.

In this uncertain context I finish writing the chapters of this book, unsure if we will ever even Burn again. Writing about community, celebration and connection from a space of confinement felt all the more poignant. In an uncanny way, had I delayed my journey across the Regionals for a few months, I would not have been able to complete it. Overnight, the book I was writing started to feel like a chronicle of how we used to gather pre-pandemic. What would lockdown mean for society and the future of community-centered movements like Burning Man?

As tends to happen in life, our personal worlds have an uncanny way of mirroring events around us, as if preparing us for the storm. For many months I had felt that the life I was leading, hurtling from place to place at breakneck speed, was unsettling me in many ways. Before the world stopped, I had thrown myself into another nomadic stint, traveling to the other side of the world. There I lost myself on Andean trails, merging onto high mountainous pathways, breathless with altitude, in constant motion, crossing borders as if they were doorways through which I could unlock pieces of my life's puzzle.

I would wake up to a changed landscape almost daily and rest in a new bed every night. The moments would stream by too fast to grasp, blurring into acceleration from the window of a speeding bus. The thrill of the new had become a way of life, and little by little the roots that tied me anywhere were coming undone. The constant movement was taking its toll and it was a challenge to stay on top of working remotely during this time, waking up at ungodly hours of the night to sit in meetings in distant time zones.

Then, just as the colorful and exuberant season of Carnival drew to a close in February, the planet suddenly and unexpectedly shifted gears. Over the course of a week, frightening events accelerated, and what seemed like a year's worth of news started to feed through our screens. Our heads reeled with information overload. Confusion surged through us like electricity, fear spreading through chatter which days before had been light-hearted, back when we took freedom for granted.

The day before confinement hit, I missed a step, running too fast down a stairwell. I would spend many months on crutches with a fractured ankle. My father in France was struck down by cancer, and started a grueling chemotherapy treatment at this difficult time. When the borders closed I stayed in France to care for him, and could not get back home to Spain for months. Meanwhile, the relationship I had left behind fell apart and I was powerless to stop it from a distance. It's as if the world was conspiring to teach me to stand still. I had to learn to walk again, and I had to sit and face pain, both my own and that of a loved one.

Everything was in turmoil, and I had reached a low point.

Everyone was affected in some way. Society shifted and an economic storm gathered. Whole industries ground to a halt or disappeared altogether. But, more alarmingly, what defined us as social beings started to break down. We were separated from each other, from touch, from smell, from the reassuring closeness of others; from those we love, but also from those we used to cross in the street but did not know. Days went by with no chance meetings, no stolen stares across a crowded train platform, no accidental brushing past a stranger. We collectively longed and ached for human contact.

All of the measures in place that warned against excessive screen time and its potential to stunt human interaction were thrown out the window. Virtual drinks, online courses and shows presented in living rooms replaced our social interactions in a matter of weeks. The speed at which this bizarre situation came to feel like the new norm shows how quickly we can adapt, and how quickly we can become accustomed to a lessening of our humanity. Every now and then there were reminders of our past lives; a familiar song, or boarding pass falling out of a pocket made us long for a time when things seemed infinitely easier.

In the backdrop the seasons changed, reminding us that in times of stillness, transformation still takes place. We had time to watch in awe as the new leaves pushed through, twisting like dancers and unfolding on bare branches until the trees popped with newly green splendor. While nature was busy with its rebirth, the cities and streets of the world fell quiet. But inside the microcosmos of our houses small revolutions took place. Through the stillness we were reminded that creativity is crucial to the human experience. Gradually blank pages filled with words, art was sketched into being, and new ideas were breathed into life.

Each individual's path has been different depending on their circumstances. While during the pandemic we weathered the same storm, as they say, we were not in the same boat. While losses to the pandemic indiscriminately cut across social barriers it was not an equal struggle. Still, this time of reflection taught all of us lessons, and we were united in a shared experience. When we finally stepped out, we realized that all this time we had not been walking alone.

Having a space to lose ourselves in as we adapt to the post-pandemic reality will be an important part of the healing process. In the aftermath of these times, we need to reconnect with models that successfully create a sense of community, and share transcendent collective experiences to help guide us through.

Before the pandemic struck, our togetherness was already being eroded for decades, through individualism, materialism and a growing "us and them" mentality. Numbed by a world where we felt more and more alienated, bombarded to consume, our generation pushed back. We collected experiences over things, we never stood still. We experienced the power of gathering, the value of having a space for escapism and play.

Burning Man was one of those playgrounds. Lost and found in these alternate realities, sucked in by the movement and its ability to create community so quickly, by the richness of experience across its global network, all quirky and welcoming in their own way. It provided a framework, a canvas for participants to shape their own world. It was for me, as it is for many, a transformational experience.

In these playgrounds we did all of our living for the year heightened and condensed into a week of sleepless days and nights. To be surrounded by an outpouring of creativity, of human possibility, made us feel alive and inspired. We were living simultaneously in a world of make-believe, but also where we could show our truest selves. Beyond the larger than life art pieces and sound systems we found wonder in small gestures. In chats with strangers over coffee, in playfulness, in exchanging hugs. We knew the importance of connection and touch, and the feeling of being in a safe space.

But, when the week's experience ended we readjusted to our old realities, leaving so many issues unaddressed. We slipped back into a world where the standard currency was to conform and consume.

When we couldn't commune in person, Burning Man brought these playgrounds into our homes through the Multiverse with a plethora of virtual events. Although they could not replace what we had lost, they offered spaces for new ways to connect, providing platforms through which we could have conversations to make sense of the present and shape our future.

Burning Man had been a space only accessible to a privileged few, and the move to a virtual space in some ways allowed for increased participation from across the world. While these spaces fell short of keeping us authentically connected, they were the in-between medium through which we could continue to commune, providing a view into the personal lives and projects of those we lived with in the dust.

Thirsty for even the faintest hit of playa magic, I logged on to the various symposia organized by Burners through Burning Man Project's Multiverse: a two-day virtual Burn, a retreat organized by Burners Without Borders, a virtual Desert Arts Preview. Whilst we sheltered in our houses, people built bridges out of isolation through collaborative initiatives and art. Projects that combined all of the creativity and playfulness that we see on the playa adapted to make sense of the challenges of the times.

The building of a Black Rock City forest project, where the artists invited participants to create trees so that we might walk among the creations of many; a giant floating iridescent wave comprised of messages of hope from participants around the world; a library to provide a space for quiet contemplation; a larger than life representation of Gaia, nurturing and magnificent. These were just a few of the art pieces in the making that would be proudly displayed on future playas.

The artworks of the past have been collaborations in terms of build, but since the pandemic, we have seen an inspirational shift in messaging, and a move toward more cumulative projects where participants around the world can contribute to the art and be part of the creative process. These projects are also being taken out of the virtual and into local communities. Much beauty will come out of this.

After the thrill of those times full of meaning traveling around Regionals, I spent months struggling to make sense of it all, numb and drained. In many ways I was still processing what all these experiences had amounted to, piecing together the flashes of memories from the journey. Perhaps the Burns didn't give us all the tools to deal with a pandemic, but it made us feel part of a community, and it motivated us to build, and bring all the creations we could dream up to life. Art is a crutch out of darkness, a way to lift ourselves and others up, replacing stagnation through creation.

As we gather again it will not just be for celebration, but also for healing. I think back to the sanctity of the temples that I experienced around the world of Burns, of their cultural differences and of the rituals which made them both a mirror of each other and unique. Their towering structures and wooden panels covered in moving messages, the pregnant silences that accompanied their burning, and the flushed faces of thousands turned towards remembrance.

We should move toward universal rituals that combine these cultural differences for healing in a meaningful way. Through this healing we can dream up a new reality, reinventing ourselves and how we commune.

Sometimes, we don't understand the magnitude of what we are living when we are in the thick of it, but as we look back, we remember the strength we summoned to make it through, like muscle memory.

It is difficult to predict with any certainty the lasting impact that the pandemic will have on our societies, and how it might shape our future. But in time, a new vision will eventually show itself. What is clear is that more than ever we need spaces to find each other, places for escapism, for dancing till dawn, for tears and laughter. As we gather again, we will burn all the brighter.

ONCE UPON A TIME IN THE DUST

Epilogue:
Going Home

*A*s the world started to stir post-pandemic, so did my need to make sense of this period of intense societal change. Although I hadn't been to a Burn for two years, its principles were etched in my psyche. I was particularly struck by the power of the temples across cultures. The cathartic relief they provide seemed to be a constant across all continents, and I had tried to convey this in the small exhibition I put up in 2019.

While much of the art of Burning Man is playful, taking time for introspection seems equally important to the Burning Man experience. 2020 was a stark reminder of this. Reporting on Burning Man culture globally and building smaller-scale art had set the stage for creating something bigger, more impactful. Following Burning Man's—and the wider world's—two-year hiatus, I felt a calling to do just that. Trying my hand at creating larger scale art seemed like a logical next step, and I was about to find out what a crazy rollercoaster ride it was, with new journeys through Mexico and Burning Man's hometown in San Francisco.

Through the process of creation, and almost five years on from starting my journey across Regionals, I started making sense of it. The memories of those times started flooding back, and its lessons crystallizing. There is another world out there, and it can be whatever we make it. With a smile I felt ready to dig out my dusty suitcase and put my foot back on the gas, taking on the final stretch of the long journey home.

After so much time surrounded by art created for its own sake, effervescent with creativity and heart, my soul was touched forever. The first time I went to Burning Man, I had avoided researching any of the art and had zero expectation of what I would find. I arrived in the middle of a dust storm. A complete and total whiteout, like being trapped in a blizzard at the top of a mountain. I could barely make out my outstretched hand, let alone realize that cloaked behind this relentless dust was the world's largest outdoor gallery.

Most of the art I had experienced up to this point had been in enclosed spaces—spaces where you lined up to be herded in single file past paintings and sculptures, often created by just a handful of recognized artists. People would nod approvingly before moving on, barely engaging with the pieces on display. Even with something as subjective as art, we tend to follow the grain.

But when we turn that paradigm on its head and move from being spectators to participants and co-creators in art, the experience changes us. As the dust curtains parted and as day turned to night my jaw dropped at the dreamscape that emerged. By sunrise I was fully immersed in this alternate reality.

Anyone who has been to Black Rock City can confirm that the creative experiment unfolding there is breathtaking. It is art on steroids. Beyond the grand structures out on playa it lines each avenue of the city in colorful camps and wacky installations, with mutant vehicles as its main public transportation system. Whatever the imagination can think up finds a place here: from giant structures like *Head Maze*, a 40-foot meditating mind, to a Mario Kart racetrack, a bike fashioned into Falkor from *The Never-Ending Story*, or a 30-person alien parade.

Within this hyper-sensory world some pieces stuck with me and lingered. I still remember the impact of the art piece *Charon* that I stumbled across riding in deep playa one frigidly cold night. There stood a monumental wheel, lined with skeletons appearing to be rowing aimlessly through the night sky. They were eerily illuminated by erratic strobe light, adding to the hypnotic scene. The wheel started spinning when people pulled the thick and dusty ropes on either side. And as they did, they became part of the art piece, activating its macabre dance to deliver its message. Dusty, white and doomed to the same destiny as the skeletal figures they brought to life.

With countless pieces of participatory art, Black Rock City is an undeniable art mecca. Various mutant vehicles take participants on daily tours, narrating selected structures on-playa. Art structures are listed in the printed WhatWhereWhen guide, which gets progressively dustier and more dog-eared as the week advances. Their sheer number makes it impossible to see them all. This encourages artists to create ever larger and more imposing pieces, reaching for the sky and vying for attention like skyscrapers in Manhattan. Art on such a scale requires equally large-scale collaboration, with whole armies of artists coming together to conceptualize, fundraise, build and tear down what they have created. This in turn creates community.

But as you have read in these pages, art takes many forms. It is in the towering pyramids and spiraling temples that make us crane our necks up to look at them in awe. But it is equally in a walnut containing a secret necklace in a field in Argentina, or a strategically placed mirror in Japan reminding us that we are seen. It is in the gifts we give each other, without expecting anything in return.

Art offers a view into how others see the world, and sometimes a chill of recognition which speaks to a deep and secret part of us. The more interactive it is, the more it sparks playfulness and joy, and the more deeply it offers outlets for healing. Some say art brings us closer to the divine because it is a manifestation of inspired states. As we build, we lose ourselves to a higher flow. This is felt all the more strongly when we know the worlds we are building will only live in a space in time before being dismantled or ceremoniously burnt to the ground.

The yearning for these ephemeral and transformative spaces has rippled beyond Black Rock City to spark a global movement wherein the Regional groups create their unique cities. These smaller settings bring you up close and personal with the artists to strengthen community cohesion. Burns are packed with more weight when you recognize the faces behind the fires.

On the last day of Fuego Austral, we formed a human chain around the Burn. This gesture celebrated each of us and the joint effort which had gone into creating this micro-city. When a city is barely 500 strong everyone actively participates in building it. As the Man finally gave in to the fire and tumbled to the ground people cheered, cried, and embraced, touched on a very personal level by what they had created and now watched turn to ash.

Across the Regionals, art mirrors culture. The logistics at Midburn are seamless, a testament to the highly organized Israeli society. Camps are put up within hours. Here I witnessed incredible displays of engineering, such as the giant camel morphing into an awesome fire breathing dragon when burned.

The art at AfrikaBurn feels earthy against the Tankwa desert. Its 2018 temple was topped by a palm leaf roof, typical of a traditional African hut. The performance art was also immersive. In a flash one could unexpectedly be mobbed by a springbok parade, or surrounded by drummers pounding out rhythmic music in full costume.

Down under in Australia, psychedelically illuminated sound camps reign supreme at Blazing Swan, but in its quieter nooks and crannies, art installations such as the *Whisper Tree* lie in wait. This ubiquitous Australian gum tree was decorated with long LED sensors that lit up in sync with passing voices, coming alive to secrets whispered.

Each Regional has its unique flavor and taps into something universal: a yearning for creation, for finding and sharing unique talents with the world, and ultimately leaving a mark. It is a clarion call to the artist within. After experiencing so much creation this call grew progressively louder in my ears.

And so, I woke up to an idea in late 2021 that kept me up all night. Every year I take a moment for introspection in remembrance of the loss I experienced as a child. I reflect on how far I have come, and the route still ahead. After so much social isolation and global loss, it seemed important to take a stand and rebuild the collective healing spaces that had been dismantled.

In my mind's eye, I saw a spiraling stairway, a metaphysical space for catharsis and reflection where participants could collectively dream up a future. Inspiration tends to be sourced directly from our subconscious. In an uncanny coincidence weeks later I was struck to recall that a vision of the stairway had appeared in a recurring dream in the early days of isolation.

Sometimes our dreams call us to action, opening doors through which our souls can reawaken.

Wide-eyed, I scanned the Burning Man Project website and realized I had just under two weeks to submit the first stage of the art grant application. In those weeks, I took the seeds of an idea and sketched it into being. With no artistic or building background I had to be resourceful. Our human networks are such that when we employ a little radical self-reliance, we usually find the help we need. I reached out to architects from my wider circle and shared the concept.

When a cause ignites you, words and emotions seem to come to the surface like a rallying cry. From this place magic happens, and collaborations are born. I suddenly had four architects rallying to the cause, and we worked on the rendering through several late nights. From unlikely beginnings, it seemed the vision could actually materialize.

The Letter of Intent is the first step of an art grant application. There is no prescribed theme or format for the art that can be submitted, it just needs to align with Burning Man's mission of art as an "interactive, participatory, shared experience of creative expression." The process is competitive and a steep learning curve for an artistic newbie, but it is equal parts thrilling. Through its grants, Burning Man Project does something that is so missing in our default world: it helps would-be artists to actualize their dreams. And through this act, it unleashes an unbridled creative flow which breathes whole cities of art into life.

Creating cities, however whimsical and temporary, comes with hard work. Teams of exceptionally talented people come together each year and dedicate considerable time, resources, and energy to build incredible feats of architecture in some of the most unforgiving environments on earth—for no monetary return.

While developing the art proposal I found myself faced with a plethora of puzzles, such as how to secure structures against punishing desert winds without digging deep in the playa floor. BRC is an architectural Rubik's Cube. While the Burning Man Project Art Department provides some guidance to artists, it very much expects you to be radically self-reliant. In the run up to the event, even the most carefully laid plans go haywire, and literal blood, sweat, and tears go into erecting the structures acting as out-of-this world backdrops to so many shiny Instagram snaps.

Each established Regional event, regardless of its size, offers art grants to its participants. Although the grant amounts are commensurate with available resources, the Regional groups make sure art stays central to their mission, supporting participants to build their versions of a dusty city. As the AfrikaBurn website states "in the dust it's the (collaborative) projects that are the headliners, and even those are largely only revealed on arrival." The various organizations merely provide the enabling environment for the participant-led experimentation to unfold.

As the Burning Japan organizer said, "When I realized that the spirit of Burning Man is more important than making huge art installations, I thought it could also be held in Japan." My firsthand experience at Burning Japan, an event smaller in size than many BRC camps, demonstrated how right she was. In this restrictive society, even a shared hug is a conscious form of communal expression. And while the art is simple, I would discover that a single meditation bed set up under a blue sky can be packed with life-changing significance for its artist.

After two intense weeks of planning—and a last-minute panic, slashing text after mixing up the character limit for a word limit—I submitted the Letter of Intent for the grant. Fast forward a month and I found myself awake at 3 a.m. on a cold December night. My heart raced in front of an unopened email from the Burning Man Project Art Department, feeling the weight of its significance. Finally, and after a deep breath, I read the first line. "Congratulations," it said. "You have been invited to submit a full proposal." And just like that I was back in acceleration mode.

Realizing I only had four weeks over the Christmas break to work on the proposal, I met with the architect to hash out next steps. This was also at the height of the Omicron variant infections which would throw many a spanner into the works. The process was made all the more challenging as it coincided with a trip to Mexico.

As fate would have it, I was connected to a Mexican architect who would eventually become instrumental in the proposal. His experience building COVID-19 hospitals and commitment to the ethos of the project would make him an ideal partner to work with. With time running out and budget questions still left to address, I traveled to San Francisco to meet construction companies for in-person discussions.

As I boarded the flight, it hit me that this was the first time in seven years that I would be in the city without attending a Burn. The San Francisco I knew was usually in the throes of pre- or post-Burn planning, and it was not hard to spot the tell-tale throngs of soon-to-be-Burners by the outlandish hats or fur coats they carried, which would get the heart fluttering for the homecoming that lay ahead.

Black Rock City has such a reach that its pilgrims pour in from all around the world leading up to the event. They appear at airports like a Burner version of *Where's Waldo* before eventually converging en masse at the gates of BRC. As I scanned the plane two years on from my last gathering the atmosphere was very different: a sea of masked faces with no fur or cheeky smiles in sight.

The next day I made the journey from San Francisco to Sausalito on a sun-drenched morning. Crossing the Golden Gate Bridge, I had flashes of the journeys I had made to the desert for five consecutive years, exhilarated as the dust beckoned. So much has happened since. But while I wouldn't be making the journey to BRC until many months later, I had a Burn Mission to carry out.

I was to meet with representatives from Rhubu, an inspirational engineering company that has worked on many Burning Man art pieces. They started the Rhubu Gives Back program during the pandemic, donating engineering services to help bring communities together. In the days that followed I would meet with leads from large camps such as Entheos and Playa

Bike Repair, and I would have conversations with Andrew Johnstone, Jerry Deal, and other incredibly skilled Burning Man artists.

Despite many of my meetings being canceled due to COVID, the in-person discussions I was able to have were worth their weight in gold. As much as we rely on online communication these days, nothing can beat face to face. It was humbling to hear stories from these giants, and to be reminded of the generosity and awe-inspiring resourcefulness of the Burning Man community.

Behind the scenes, artists face monumental logistical challenges to bring structures out to the desert. There are multiple hurdles along the way when pre-building off site; transportation, assembly out in BRC, making sure structures are safe, and leaving no trace. Thinking through each of these steps myself gave me a whole new appreciation for the level of effort and the epic collaborations involved.

While building art in Black Rock City has probably the most complex requirements, bringing art to each of the Regionals comes with its own challenges. The rocky route leading to the Tankwa desert at AfrikaBurn is infamous for shredding tires, with cars and trucks frequently breaking down. At Nowhere out in Spain the ground is sloped, which adds a layer of complexity for builds. Any art brought on site also needs to be dismantled and stored after the event due to the no-burn policy in the Monegros desert. This translates into far fewer large-scale art structures on site. At Blazing Swan artists are largely limited to sourcing materials in Perth, one of the most isolated cities in the world, and have to share their build site with the array of bugs that call the outback home, not least its omnipresent flies.

On my final day in San Francisco, I was connected to the team who built the Mayan Warrior from its beginnings in 2012 to the playa legend that it is today. After my Regional experiences it felt fitting to bring art from another country, and I decided to build my piece in Mexico. On arrival, I headed straight to one of the Mayan Warrior fundraisers.

Entering the Warrior's belly, I felt the bass purr as soon as I stepped into the fold. The art car pulsated with its thousand lights, all the more imposing in a smaller setting off-playa. It incorporates the "Eye of God"—*Tzicuri*—from the Wixárika culture, a symbol of the union between man, nature and the energies that surround both. With warm sand beneath our feet and the laser-filled Mayan night above we danced as if the world had never stopped, and those around us had always been by our side. I finally felt the magic of the Burn after two long years.

A few days later I submitted the proposal, entrusting it into the hands of fate. Regardless of the outcome, I believe the best stories are written outside of our comfort zones. I embarked on this ride with no artistic experience, and in two months was launched into a crash course, reconnecting with the community that had inspired me. Too often we think of art as the end result, but art is a journey in itself. From the beautiful moment when inspiration strikes, through giving the idea space to germinate, to the times of reflection that intersperse creation; the path to completion is far from linear. Setbacks are lessons we are given along the way. Building seems like the logical next step on my Burn quest, a rite of passage that I worked up to, internalizing the principles until they came to the fore in artistic creation.

As psychiatrist Pierre Janet put it, "Every life is a piece of art, put together with all means available." Burning Man has a way of turning our lives into art the moment we step onto its rollercoaster and become active participants in its experiment. There is no act too small, and whatever we choose to gift has a ripple effect. Creation fosters creation.

Our default world champions conformity and consumerism and actively discourages us from pursuing our creative talents. But Burning Man lets us reconnect to the artist within. Art—in all its forms—is the thread that unites its global movement. There is a reason why, despite cultural differences, Burning Man art has a characteristic feel regardless of where it is built. It is the manifestation of one people guided by common principles. The playas of the world are every shade of their citizens, joined in collective effort to build cities out of dust. In the words of Larry Harvey, people come for the art, they stay for the community.

After this two year pause the time has come to go home. Reflecting on what I have experienced, it is no understatement to say that since embarking on this journey across the Regional Network I have emerged transformed, a new version of myself. A soon-to-be published author, an aspiring artist—and an expert at conjuring up playful outfits with very few accessories. As a child I would write stories and poems, and lose myself to imaginary worlds for hours. Later, trapped in the routine of the grind I felt like I had lost my way. I stopped writing and I stopped dreaming. Entering the Burning Man world turned my perception of what was possible on its head. It forced me to look inward during the process, opening up deep rooted wounds of the past that would otherwise have stayed buried.

During what I call *My Burn Year* I put everything on the line, a complete reset and departure from all that I had built so far. I knew that I wanted to write about the journey, but I didn't have a clue what would come of it. I wrote the manuscript with no expectations, not even knowing whether there would ever be another Burn in the early stages of the pandemic. It was only over two years later once I'd finished the first draft that I was by chance connected with the Burning Man publishing team.

For all the fun I had (and it was a BLAST) there were countless moments when I felt lonely far from home, dirty from not showering for a week, and exhausted, cursing the relentless music playing near my tent. Times when society made me question my life choices and why I still hadn't settled down in my mid-thirties, or when my dwindling bank balance made me wonder what the hell I was doing. Juggling work alongside the journey often felt like having a split personality. But damn it felt good to be alive.

Midway through my journey, after Midburn, I felt a shift in my ability to engage with people. In the city grind I had experienced some level of functional depression, but when we put down our phones and talk to the strangers around us we live more purposefully. I started having more meaningful exchanges, across all age groups. A good rule to live by is to always speak to the eldest (and preferably dustiest) person in the room—they have the best stories and can teach you a thing or two about life.

In the end I made more meaningful connections in that year than I can count, and the tribe I originally found at BRC in Nevada now extends around the world, all of them with that hint of eccentricity that seems to be a fixture of Burners. I can attest to the fact that the magic and transformational experiences that I was blown away by at my first Burn are replicated a hundred times over across the Regional Network, simply because the magic is authentically gifted by the participants that make up each of these temporal cities, regardless of size or location. The connections I was lucky to make have withstood distance, time and a global pandemic. They have inspired me to think big. Looking forward, I plan to create art for collective healing, and try to figure out how to apply the lessons of community building to my social development work.

There is no doubt that Burning Man has grown from strength to strength after a two year pause. You can cancel an event, but you can't cancel a movement. If anything, this timeout has just made Burning Man stronger. It has also pulled into sharp focus the need for Regionals to be more easily accessible and sustainable around the world. The fact that it survived through the generous donations of its followers, and the huge number of online symposiums and events that were held during this time to reflect on Burning Man's future are a testament to this. When the stakes were high, it rose higher with a joyous battle cry.

Regionals started the charge, navigating uncertainty and hosting events post-pandemic such as Miami's Love Burn in February 2022. The outpouring of creativity, wonder and love from its connection-starved participants was all the more breathtaking. New Regionals have also mushroomed out of this time of stillness, including groups in places off the beaten track like Nam Burn in Namibia. The family is extending outwards. And let us not forget that Burners Without Borders continued its work in community resilience throughout this hiatus. For instance, Burners organized to gather, albeit virtually, to donate personal protective equipment such as masks for hospitals and others in need at the height of the pandemic.

Nearly five years on from starting my journey, the world feels even more disconnected. We are perennially glued to our screens scrolling through videos of baby hedgehogs or *insert cute animal of choice* and bombarded with ads as we do. The film *Don't Look Up*, meant as a parody of our times, feels more like a documentary. Burning Man is obviously not the ultimate panacea for this, but it does offer a space where people can unplug and have actual conversations, beyond the—undoubtedly epic—partying that it is known for. And why not have it all? Partying and philosophizing in a LED-illuminated *Wizard of Oz* lion costume sounds great to me. The important thing is that in this space, we the participants create what matters to us. "We build the hive, they bring the honey," as Larry Harvey once said.

Some dismay that Burning Man has become "too mainstream," but is that really a bad thing? Why wouldn't we thrust a movement that champions values that we should live by like Radical Inclusion, Decommodification and Leaving No Trace further into the limelight? With more eyes on it there will also be higher accountability for Burning Man to really stand behind its values. It's high time we moved from a transactional to a relational society, and the events we have lived through during the pandemic have just served to drive this home in big neon lights. The future of Burning Man is to act as a beacon for what could be, a pressure cooker for a more human centered society. The spread of the Regional Network has made it more accessible, allowing more people to participate in the social experiment, each giving it their own unique weird and wonderful local flavor.

The time is ripe for more shenanigans across the Burning Man world. We can't wait to lose ourselves to its cities once more…

Covered in dust and trinkets, cycling to the sunrise, golden smiles all around. Hundreds of hands rising in fur coats as the flaming sun finally peers over the desert peaks, emblazoning the dead-still Black Rock playa and its towering artworks, banishing the frigid night. The lazy morning stretch in the tall grass of the pampa at Fuego Austral, passing round the mate pot while wrapped in thick blankets and the chatter of newfound friends. The midday sun at Midburn sizzling like a mirage over the Negev desert and its bearded wanderers, a golden camel rising on its hind legs in the distance as if in flight. The stifling late afternoon heat of Nowhere, alive with glistening naked painted bodies. The sunsets of a hundred shades at AfrikaBurn casting shadows on glowing faces, on the earthy soil and wooden art pieces, before giving way to the bejeweled African night. The distant mist rising from the packed sauna of Burning Japan to mix with the cool night air, deep in the autumnal valley. The tangle of electronic beats and vibrations from a thousand feet that shake through the Australian bush till the early hours at Blazing Swan.

The experience will be whatever we make of it.

Will you help write the next chapter?

It's time to go HOME!

Acknowledgements

This book began as a desire to immerse myself in the Burner world near and far, to understand how this unique community replicates itself in widely different environments. I'm happy to report the antidote to our disconnected societies can be found across all continents—it is within us all.

I am grateful for all the people who showed me this truth along the way. I traveled to almost all of the Burns alone and came out of each with a newfound family. Without their open hearts, this adventure could not have taken place. It is impossible to name all those I met along the way, but some of the most unforgettable are below.

First and foremost to the people of my life who stood by me every step of the way. The best family I could wish for, my talented Dad Graham, who created beautiful illustrations of the different Regionals I attended; my amazing sister Amanda and mother Liz, and nieces Elina and Ines. To the man I have shared most of my life with, Guillermo Granell, the first ever Spanish Ranger. My forever on and off playa family Jessica and Michael Cerasi. I love you all very much.

Fuego Austral: Sebastian Muro, whom I started the journey with packed into his grandmother's tiny car. My *esposa* June Heiras who was sent to me by the gods. The colorful Aaron Christopher who I found trapped in a onesie. The *Barrilete* crew led by the cosmic Julian. To the tireless Fuego Austral organizer Ignacio Roizman, and Fernando Regalado. Gauchos with big hearts.

AfrikaBurn: my partner in crime in this and so many life adventures, Sophie Mohammed. Howie Gasman, who truly appreciated my alien artwork and provided valuable feedback on some of the chapters. Leatt Bohot, the world is fruitier when you are in it. Amrisha Prashar for her special friendship and stew. To Lorraine Tanner and the Outreach crew for the amazing community work they do in the Tankwa and all the help with my camp set up.

Midburn: Dean Pogs, who shared in the magic and misadventures at Midburn and beyond. Nir Melamed for our special coffee times. Itay and Hagar Waisman who showed me timeless love at their wedding, and their newborn child. Cas Feder, one of the Midburn organizers who I unfortunately never managed to meet in person but who helped with Midburn logistics.

Nowhere: Daniel Sanson and his incredible camp set up, and Viktor Sanchez his campmate. Justin Richmond-Decker, who fell in love out in the middle of Nowhere and connected three regional Burn experiences for me. My extended Nowhere family and Barcelona besties Gemma Bonner, Stef Decamps and Larriza Gayla Garcia, whose friendship I treasure.

BRC: Gerard Caballa, who has been there since my first Burn and is truly one of a kind. The legend that is Eric Ensign, aka the Dude, and our search for the elusive question. Ayala Talpai, the sweet Druid soul who officiated my playa wedding. Santa, aka Jim Bertsch, for keeping the spirit of Christmas alive through the years. Campmates from Entheos and AmaZone. Frank Rodriguez, Yvette, Marisol and our extended US Burner group. Bastiaan Bas, for our long on and off playa chats. My Costco soulmate, Connor McClelland.

Burning Japan: To the wonderful Burning Japan organizer Maki Oshita and all the advice she provided. Tyler Carrico and all the members of the brotherhood. Coleen the Weasel Queen and the vulnerability she showed in her fortune telling tent. Satoshi Yogo, who drove us out to the site and shared his life-changing meditation tent experience.

Blazing Swan: Christian Denham, a true character who owes me the recipe to his mystery juice. Yoann Degioanni, the musically talented zebra, and all the Treetops crew. Gabby Hun, for the heart-to-heart conversations.

Clint Franklin for the laughs. Tim Braybrooke for teaching me the basics about utes. The Blaze organizer Damon Pages-Oliver, who gave me the event backstory over dinner one night.

To those who lent their voice for the temple art exhibition; Fuego Austral: Ignacio Roizman; AfrikaBurn: Howie Gasman, Leatt Bohott; Midburn: Alon Landa; Nowhere: Guillermo Granell; BRC: Eric Ensign; Burning Japan: Maki Oshita; Blazing Swan: Yoann Degioanni, Tom.

A special thanks also goes to Jennifer Raiser who put me in touch with the Burning Man editorial team and helped the dream come true. The legendary Andie Grace who was there every step of the way, as well as Stuart Mangrum and Molly Vikart who provided critical editorial guidance. Superstar Kirsten Weisenburger, and Dominique Debucquoy-Dodley for their communication support. Michael Vav for his guidance and friendship. And last but not least Steven Raspa for his insights and leadership of the Regional Network.

Photo Credits

Introduction: Guillermo Granell

Fuego Austral: Sebastian Muro

AfrikaBurn: Roxane Jessi

Midburn: Oren Cohen

Nowhere: Roxane Jessi

BRC: Guillermo Granell

Japan Burn: Anne Mare

Blazing Swan: Roxane Jessi

Pandemic: Roxane Jessi

Going Home: Guillermo Granell

Author Image: Marta Pilotto

About the Author

Roxane Jessi has spent her life exploring communities around the world, traveling to 60+ countries. Her career has been anything but conventional, working on Congolese police reform, Iraqi counterterrorism, and women's rights in Africa. Disillusioned with our disconnected societies, she had an "aha moment" during her first Burning Man sunrise. She became fascinated with how Burning Man manifests across cultures, eventually embarking on a yearlong around-the-world

tour of seven Burn events to find out. She worked her day job throughout, alternating between suits and tutus while trying to stay sane. A lover of imaginary worlds as a child, she could be found writing poems in class hoping that one day her words might inspire others. She typically spends a quarter of the Burn rummaging for *insert missing object* in her tent/bag and the rest lost on solo missions.